RECORDED VERSIONS
GUITAR

AUTHENTIC TRANSCRIPTIONS
WITH NOTES AND TABLATURE

switchfoot
the Beautiful Letdown

Music transcriptions by David Stocker and Jeff Story

ISBN 0-634-09295-2

HAL•LEONARD®
CORPORATION

7777 W. BLUEMOUND RD. P.O. BOX 13819 MILWAUKEE, WI 53213

Visit Hal Leonard Online at
www.halleonard.com

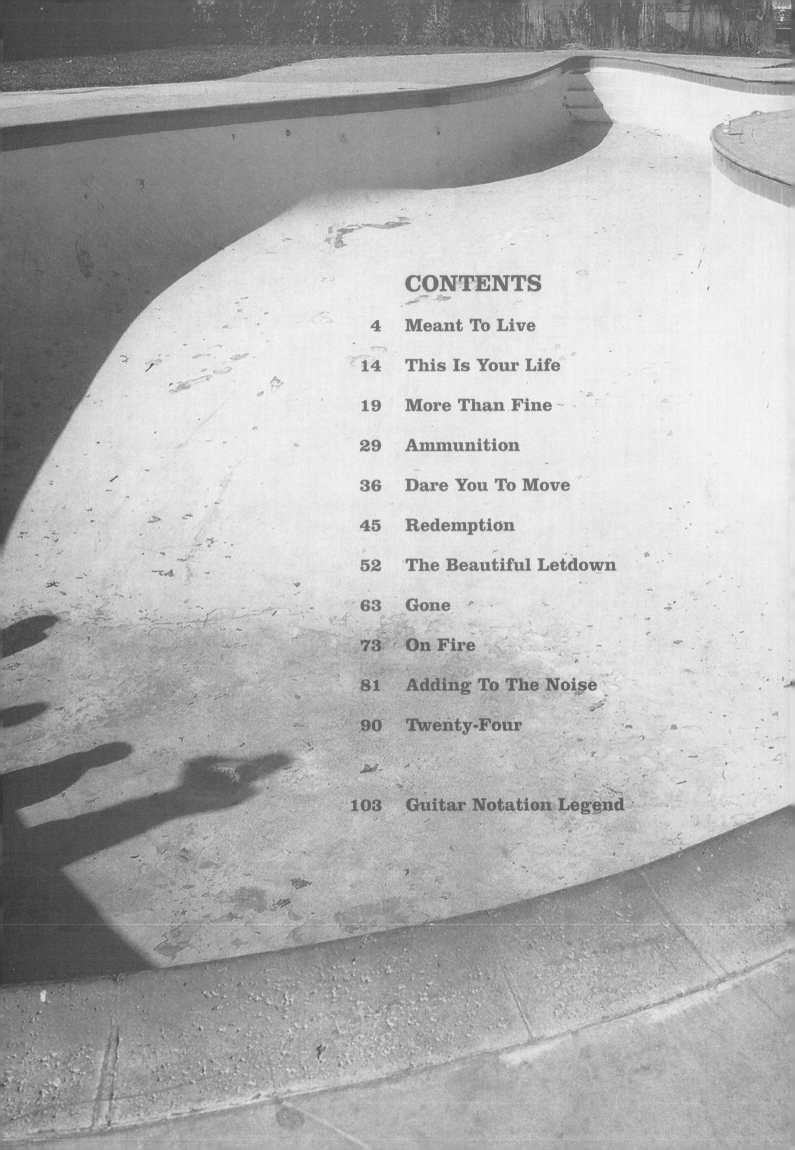

CONTENTS

Meant to Live

Words and Music by Jonathan Foreman and Tim Foreman

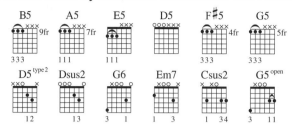

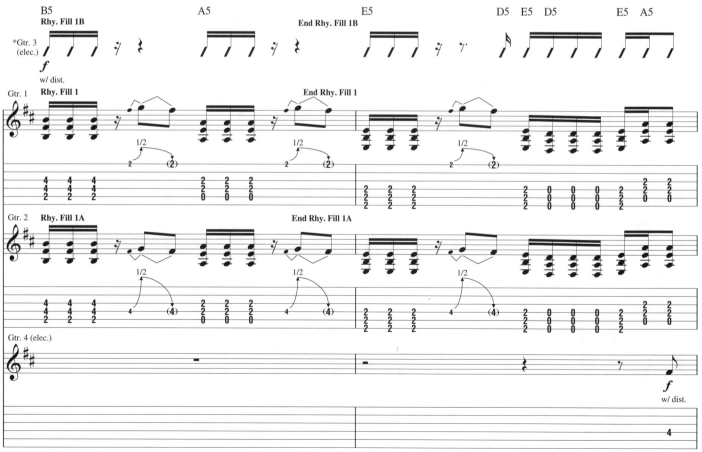

*Doubled throughout.

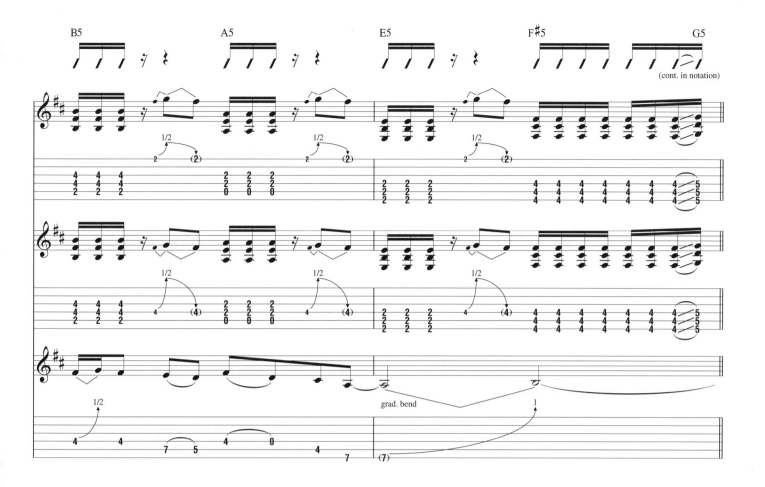

Verse

2nd time, Gtr. 4 tacet

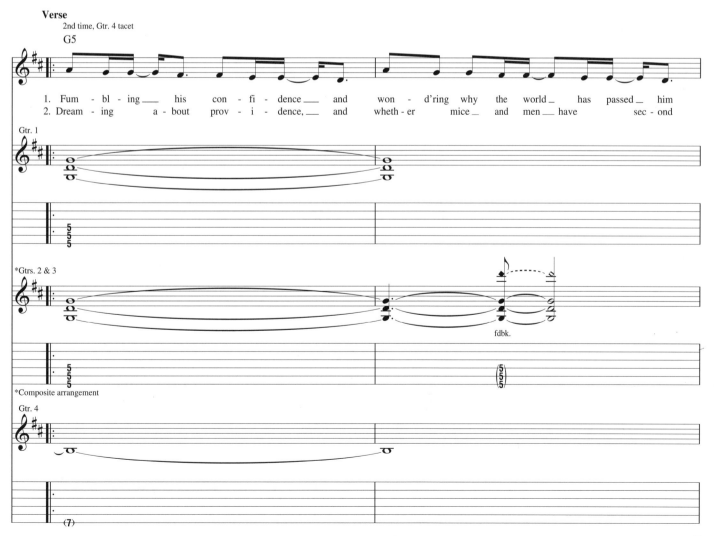

1. Fum - bl - ing ___ his con - fi - dence ___ and won - d'ring why the world ___ has passed ___ him
2. Dream - ing a - bout prov - i - dence, ___ and wheth - er mice ___ and men ___ have sec - ond

*Gtrs. 2 & 3

*Composite arrangement

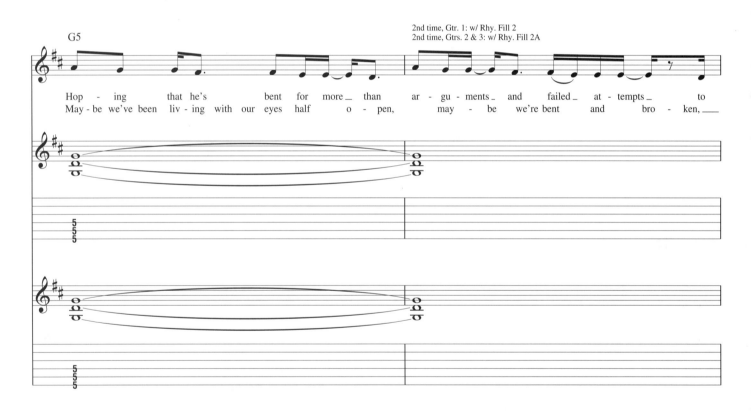

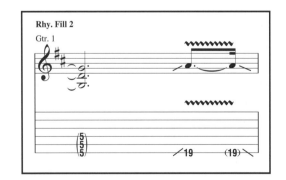

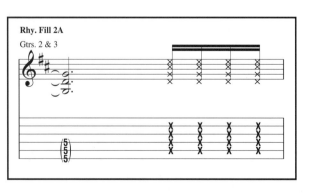

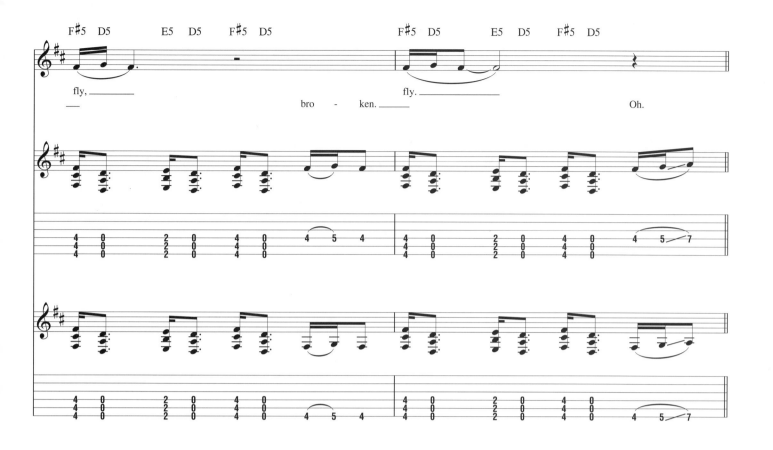

fly, _____
— bro - ken. _____ fly. _____ Oh.

Chorus

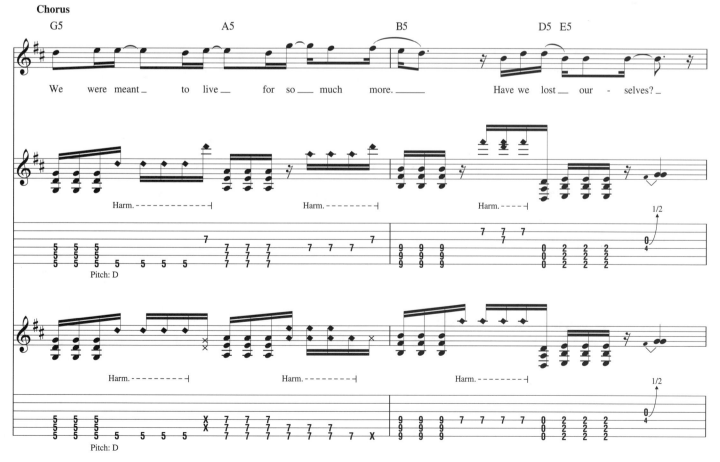

We were meant_ to live_ for so_ much more. _____ Have we lost_ our - selves? _

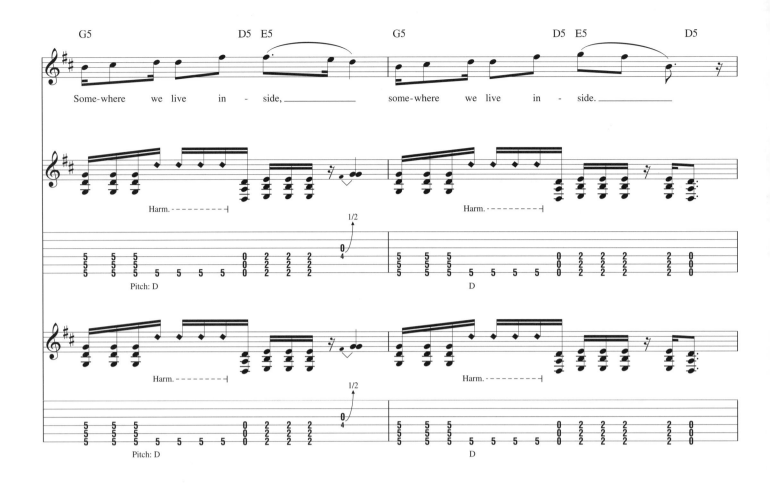

Some-where we live in - side, _____ some-where we live in - side. _____

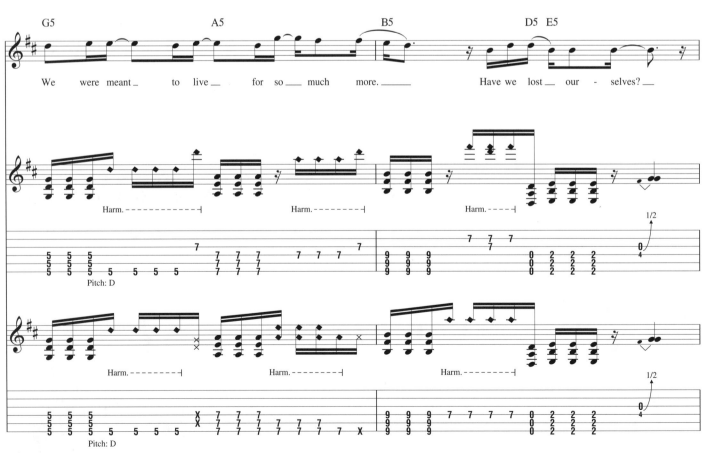

We were meant _ to live _ for so ___ much more. _____ Have we lost ___ our - selves? __

Some-where we live in - side.

Pitch: D

Harm.

Pitch: D

(2nd time, Gtr. 3 cont. in slashes)

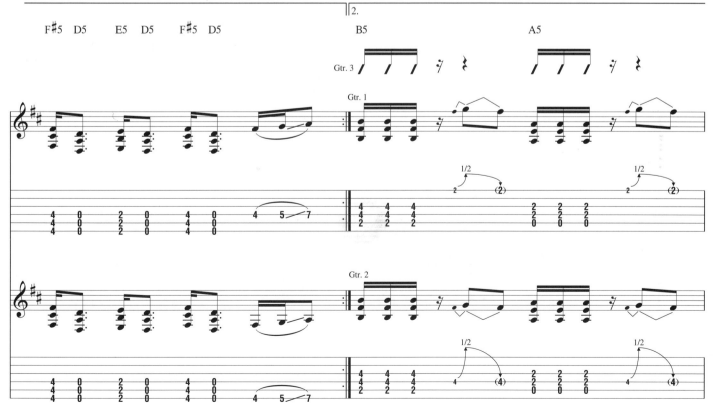

Gtr. 3

Gtr. 1

Gtr. 2

1/2

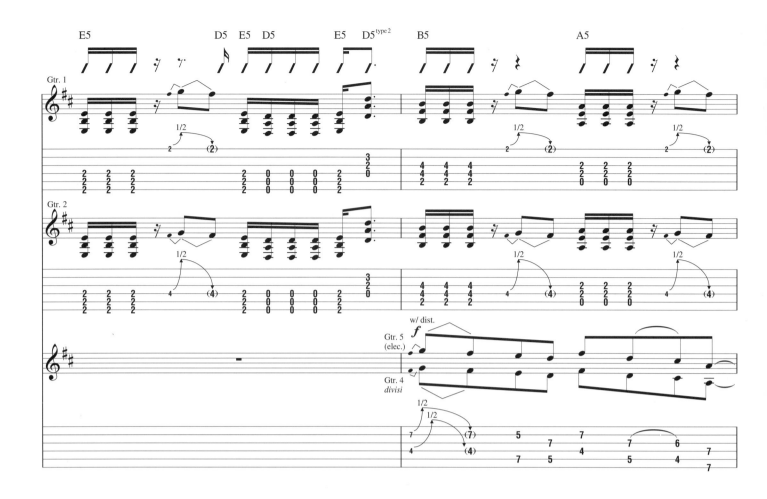

Bridge

Gtrs. 4 & 5 tacet

Rhy. Fig. 4

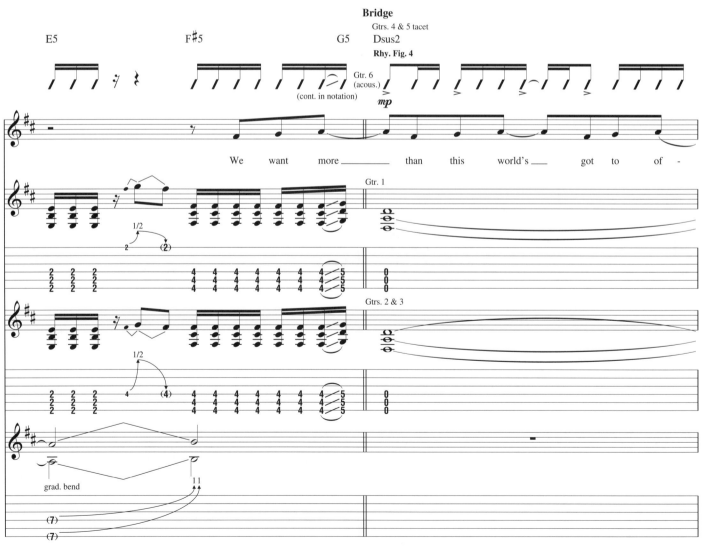

We want more _____ than this world's _____ got to of -

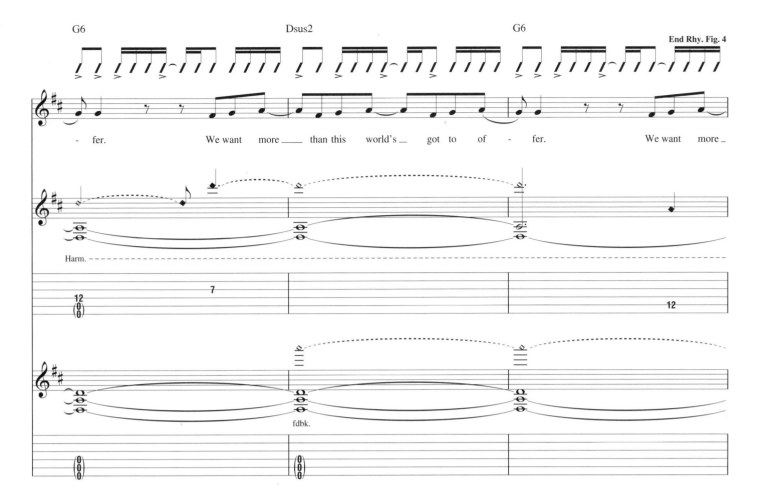

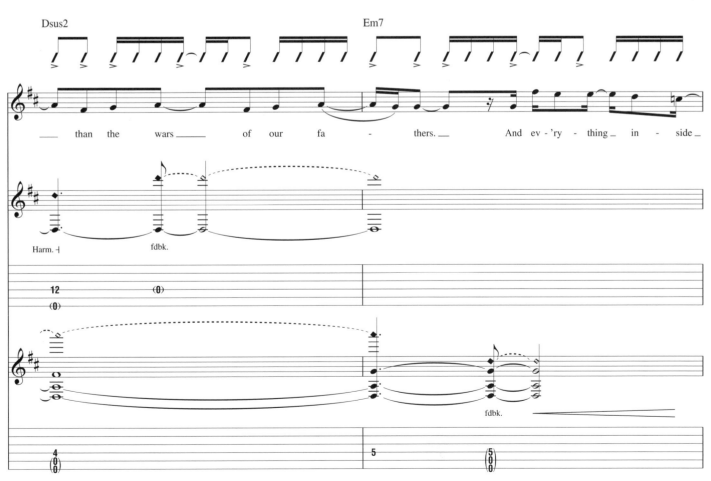

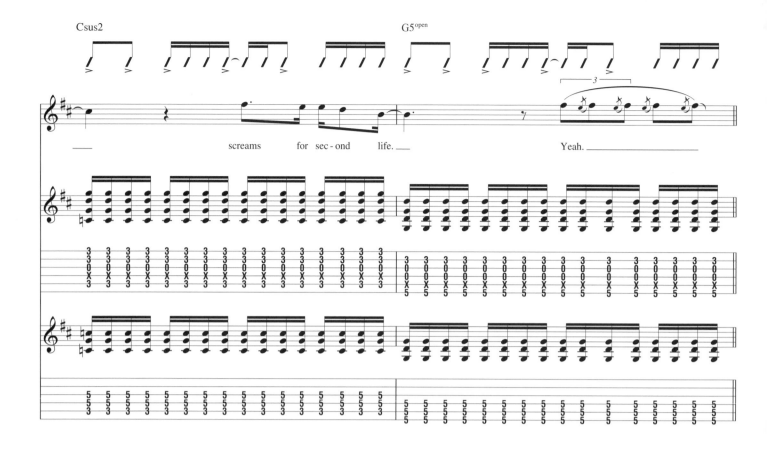

screams for sec - ond life. ___ Yeah. _____

Outro-Chorus

Gtr. 6 : w/ Rhy. Fig. 4 (2 times)

Dsus2   G6

We were meant ___ to live ___ for so ___ much more. ___ Have we lost ___ our - selves? ___

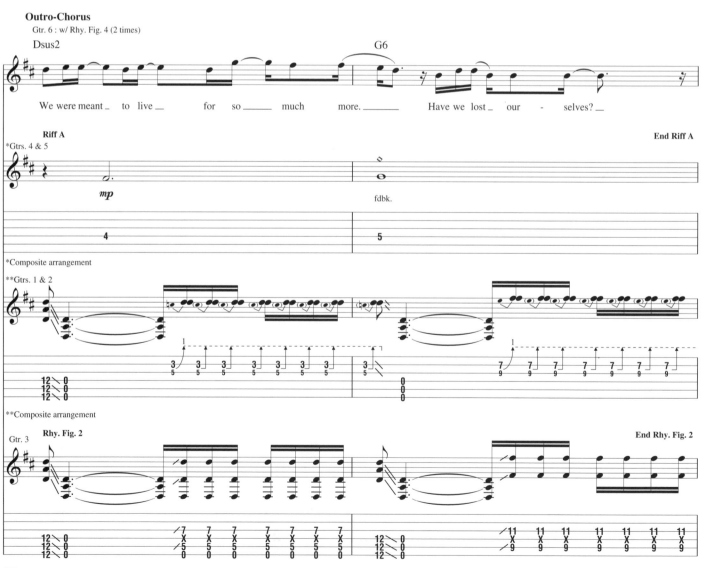

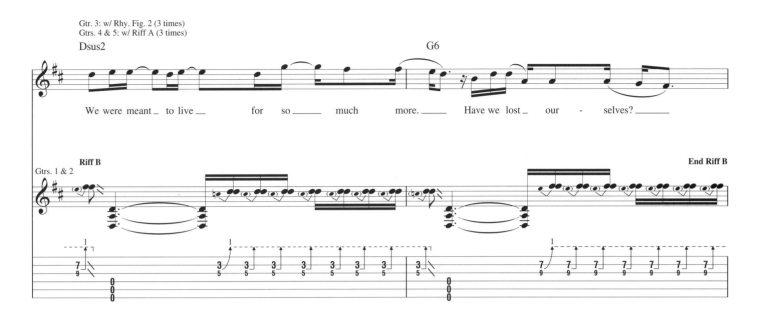

Gtr. 3: w/ Rhy. Fig. 2 (3 times)
Gtrs. 4 & 5: w/ Riff A (3 times)

Dsus2   G6

We were meant _ to live _ for so ___ much more. ___ Have we lost _ our - selves? _____

Riff B   End Riff B

Gtrs. 1 & 2

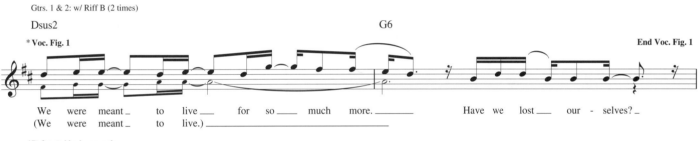

Gtrs. 1 & 2: w/ Riff B (2 times)

Dsus2   G6

* Voc. Fig. 1   End Voc. Fig. 1

We were meant _ to live _ for so ___ much more. ___ Have we lost _ our - selves? _
(We were meant _ to live.) _____

*Refers to bkgd. voc. only.

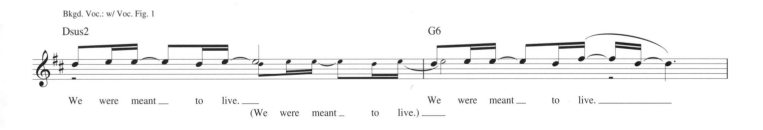

Bkgd. Voc.: w/ Voc. Fig. 1

Dsus2   G6

We were meant __ to live. __   We were meant __ to live. _____
(We were meant _ to live.) _____

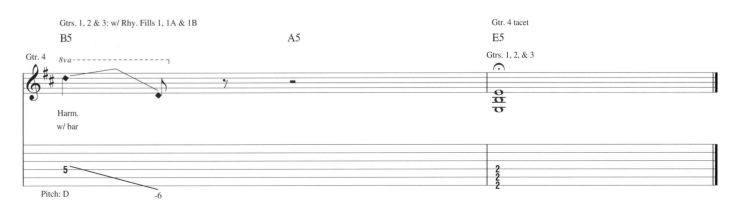

Gtrs. 1, 2 & 3: w/ Rhy. Fills 1, 1A & 1B   Gtr. 4 tacet

B5   A5   E5

Gtr. 4   8va ---------------------   Gtrs. 1, 2, & 3

Harm.
w/ bar

Pitch: D   -6

This Is Your Life

Words and Music by Jonathan Foreman

Gtr. 1: Drop D tuning, down 1/2 step:
(low to high) D♭-A♭-D♭-G♭-B♭-E♭

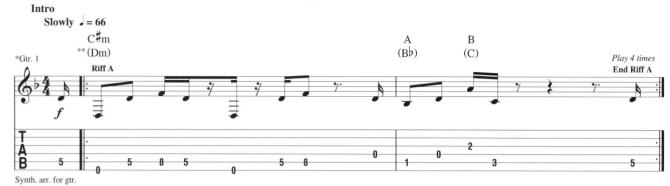

Synth. arr. for gtr.

**Symbols in parentheses represent chord names respective to detuned guitar.
Symbols above reflect actual sounding chords. Chord symbols reflect overall harmony.

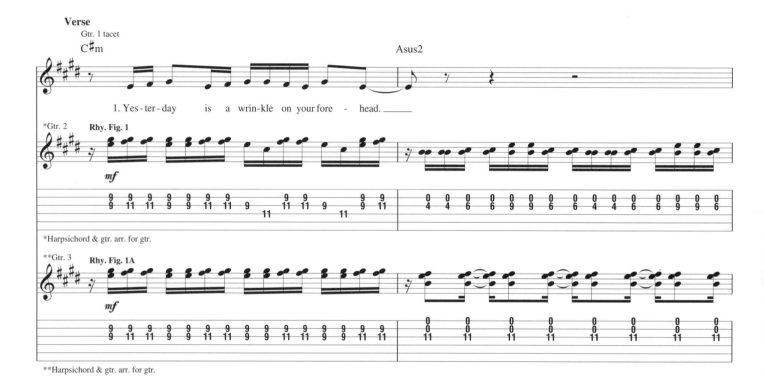

*Harpsichord & gtr. arr. for gtr.

**Harpsichord & gtr. arr. for gtr.

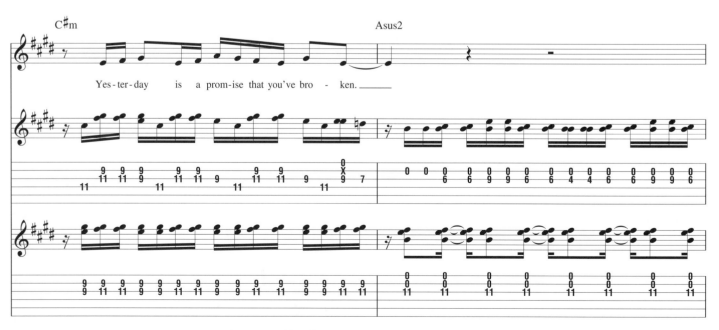

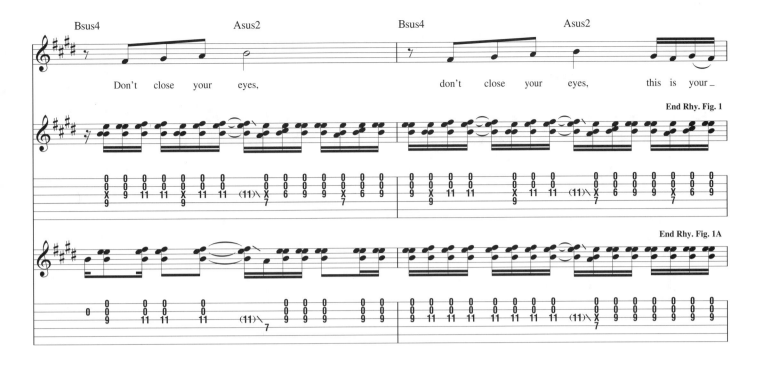

Don't close your eyes, don't close your eyes, this is your _

End Rhy. Fig. 1

End Rhy. Fig. 1A

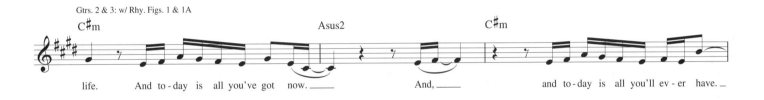

Gtrs. 2 & 3: w/ Rhy. Figs. 1 & 1A

C#m   Asus2   C#m

life. And to-day is all you've got now. _____ And, _____ and to-day is all you'll ev-er have. _

Asus2   Bsus4   Asus2   Bsus4   Asus2

Don't close your eyes, don't close your eyes. This is your _

Chorus

E   Bsus4   Asus2

life, are you who _ you want _ to be? _____ This is your _

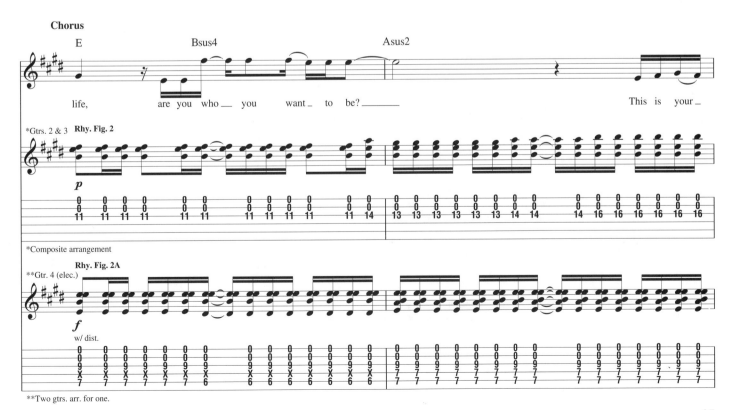

*Gtrs. 2 & 3   **Rhy. Fig. 2**

p

*Composite arrangement

Rhy. Fig. 2A
**Gtr. 4 (elec.)

f

w/ dist.

**Two gtrs. arr. for one.

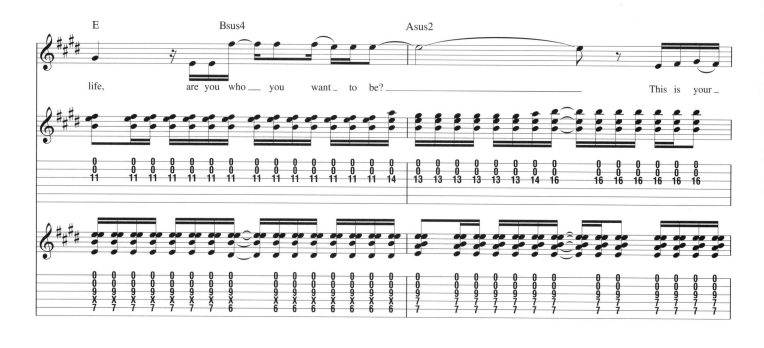

life, are you who __ you want _ to be? _____ This is your _

life, is it ev - 'ry - thing _ you dreamed it _____ would be _ when the world was young-

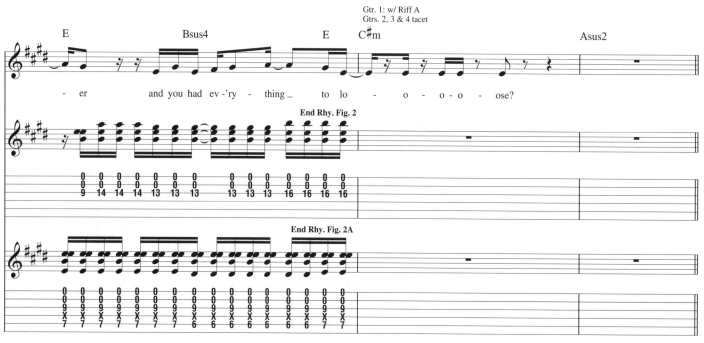

- er and you had ev -'ry - thing _ to lo - o - o - o - ose?

Verse
Gtr. 1: w/ Riff A (2 times)
Gtrs. 2 & 3: w/ Rhy. Figs. 1 & 1A (1st 4 meas.)

2. Yes-ter-day is a kid in the cor - ner. ____ Yes-ter-day is dead and o - ver. __

Chorus
Gtrs. 2 & 3: w/ Rhy. Fig. 2
Gtr. 4: w/ Rhy. Fig. 2A

And this is your __ life, are you who __ you want __ to be? __

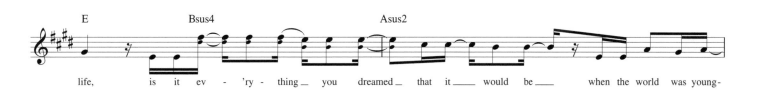

____ This is your __ life, are you who __ you want __ to be? _____ This is your __

life, is it ev - 'ry - thing __ you dreamed __ that it ____ would be __ when the world was young-

Interlude
Gtrs. 2 & 3: w/ Rhy. Figs. 1 & 1A

- er and you had ev - 'ry - thing __ to lose? ____

Don't close your eyes, don't close your eyes,

Gtrs. 2 & 3: w/ Rhy. Figs. 1 & 1A (last 2 meas.)

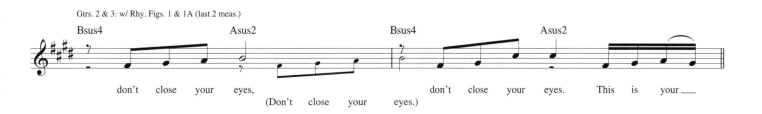

don't close your eyes, don't close your eyes. This is your ____
(Don't close your eyes.)

Chorus

life, are you who __ you want __ to be? ____ This is your __ life, are you who __ you want __ to be? __

17

More Than Fine

Words and Music by Jonathan Foreman

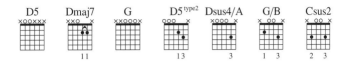

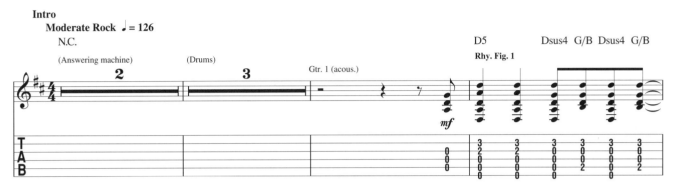

Drop D tuning:
(low to high) D-A-D-G-B-E

Intro

Moderate Rock ♩ = 126

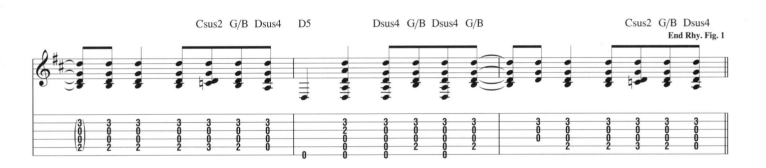

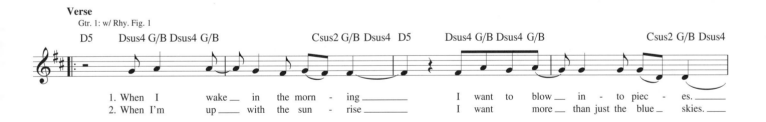

Verse

Gtr. 1: w/ Rhy. Fig. 1

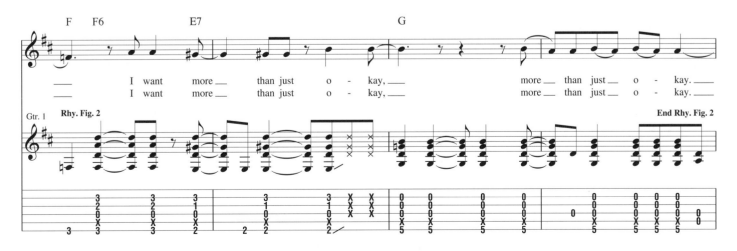

1. When I wake __ in the morn - ing _____ I want to blow __ in - to piec - es. _____
2. When I'm up __ with the sun - rise _____ I want more __ than just the blue __ skies. _____

__ I want more __ than just o - kay, __ more __ than just __ o - kay. __
__ I want more __ than just o - kay, __ more __ than just __ o - kay. __

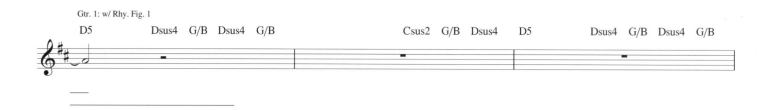

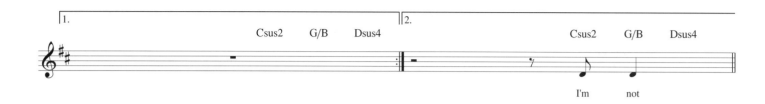

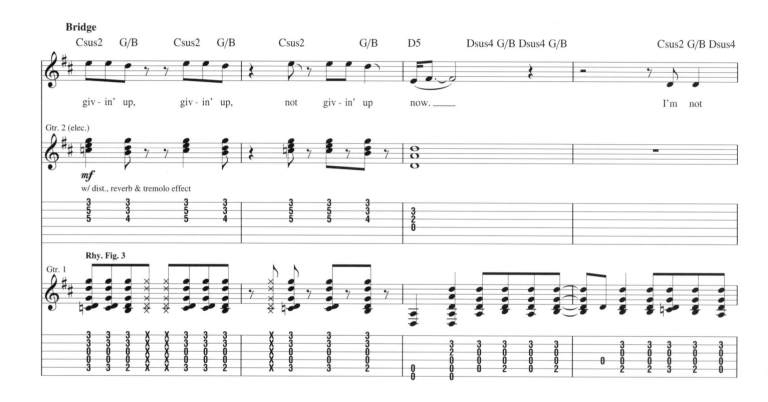

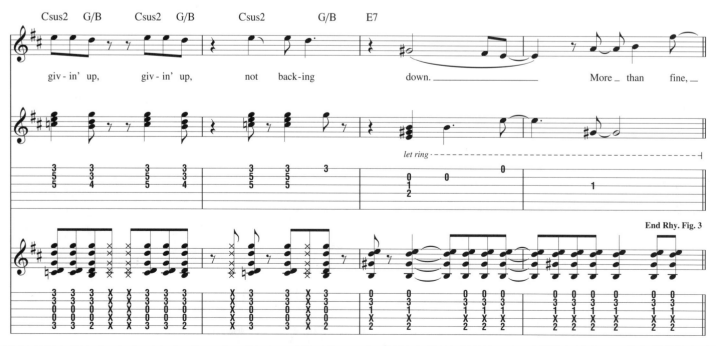

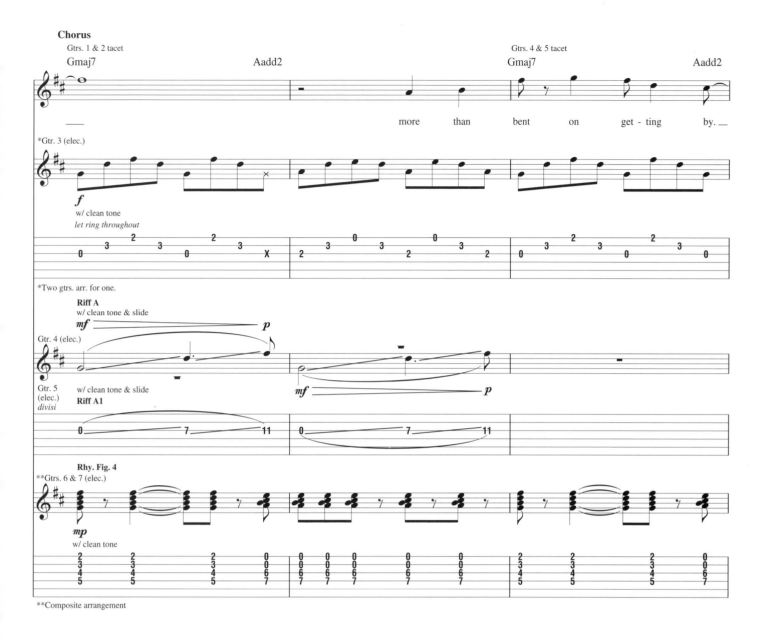

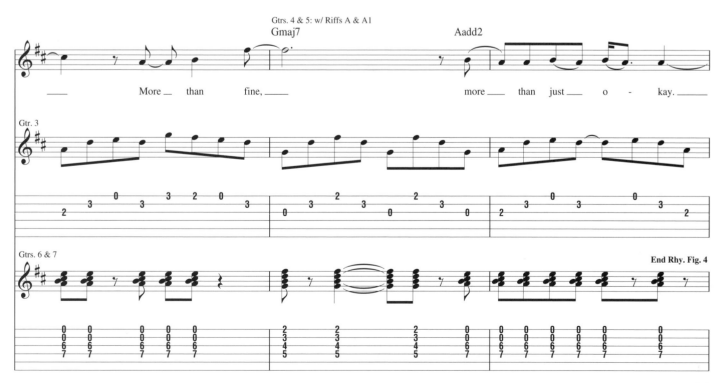

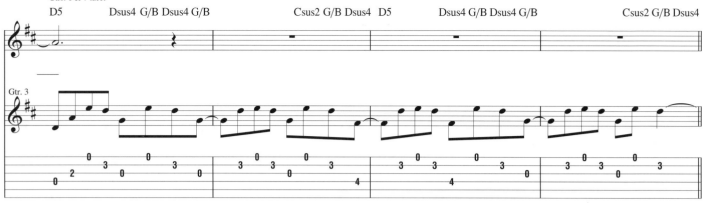

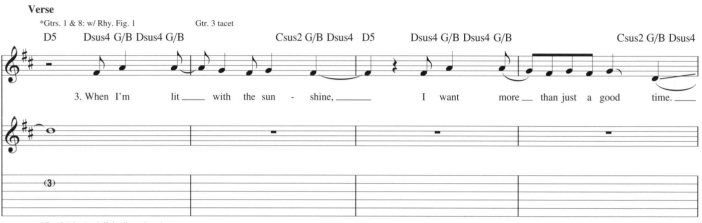

*Gtr. 8 (elec.) w/ slight dist., played *mp* .

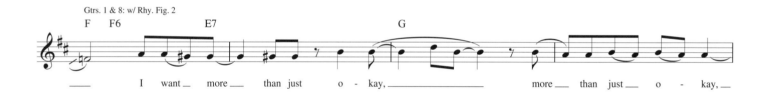

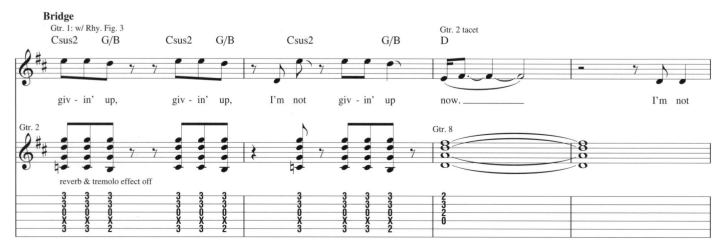

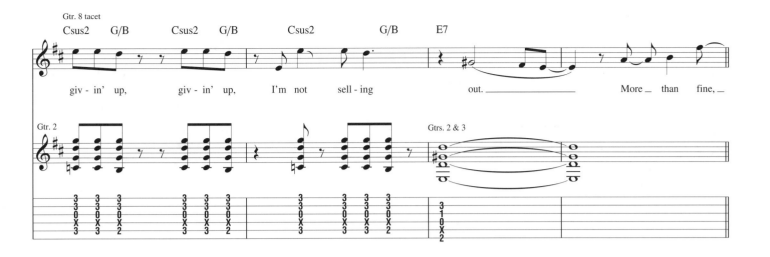

Chorus

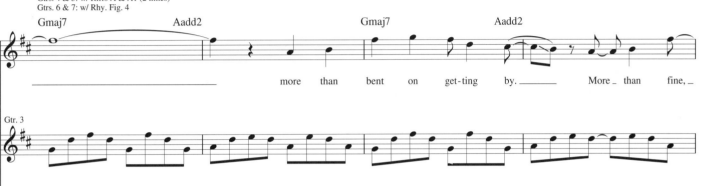

*Chord symbols reflect implied harmony.

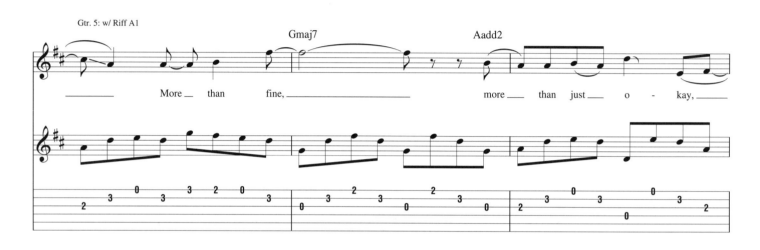

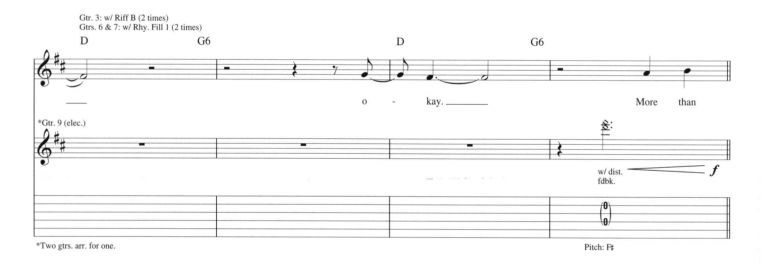

*Two gtrs. arr. for one.

Pitch: F♯

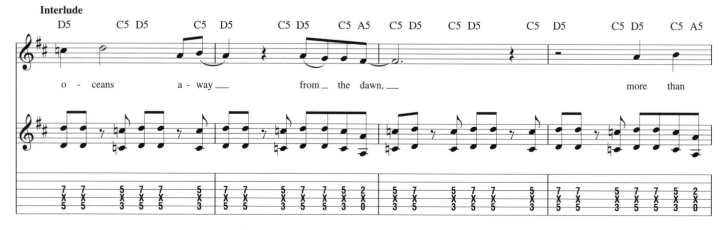

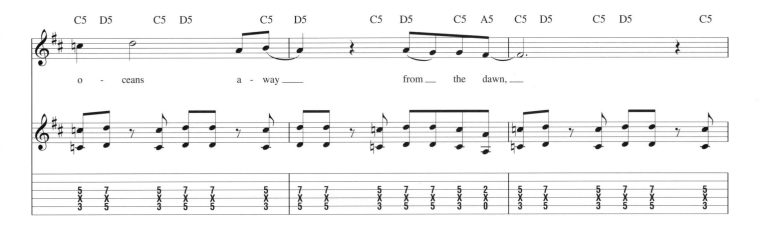

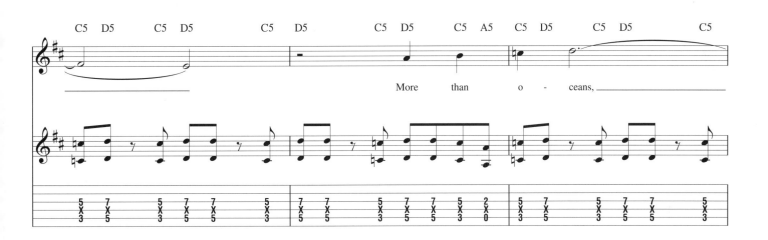

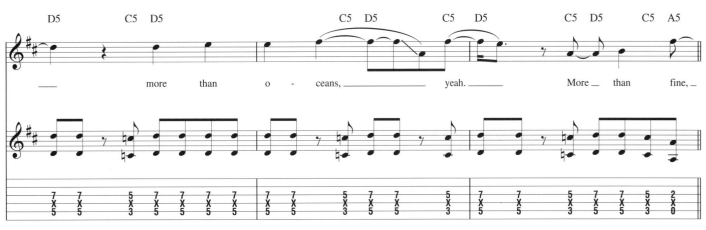

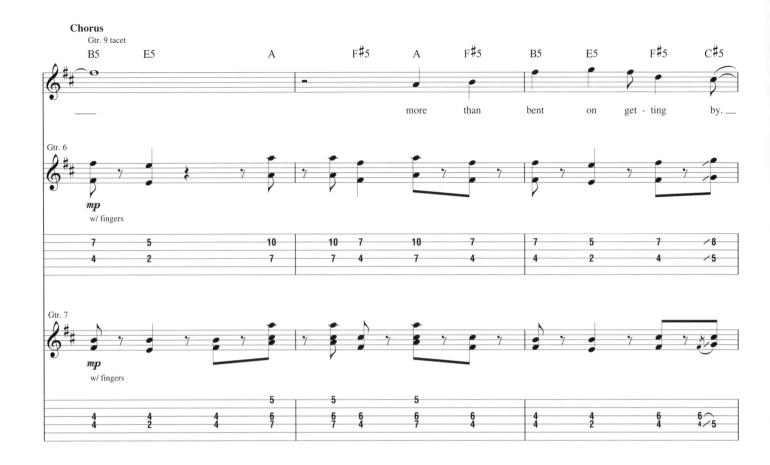

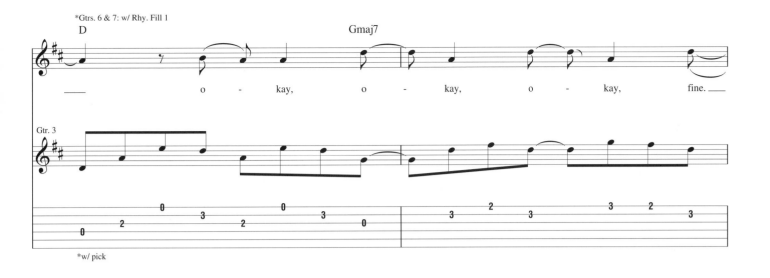

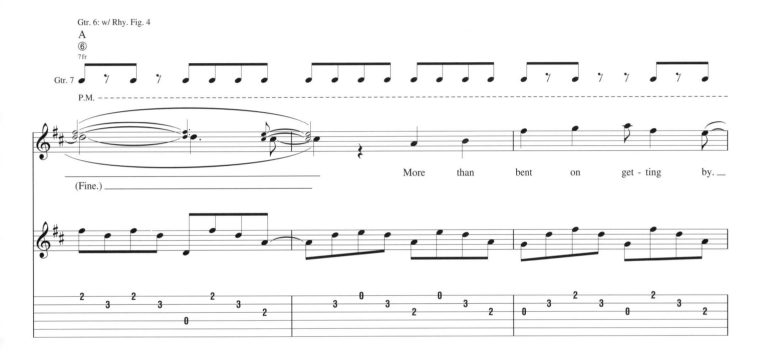

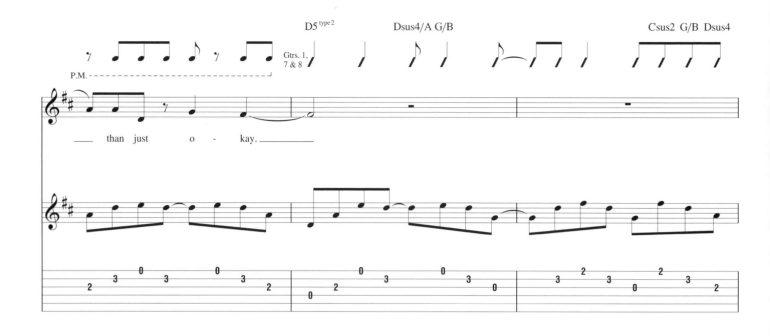

than just o - kay. ___

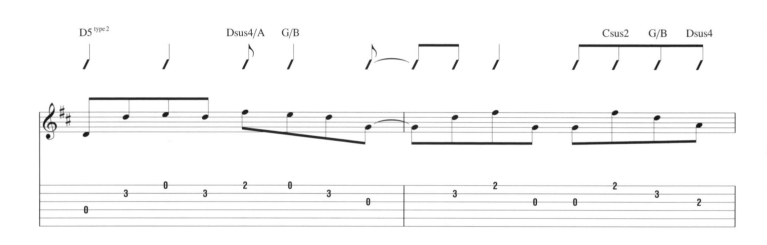

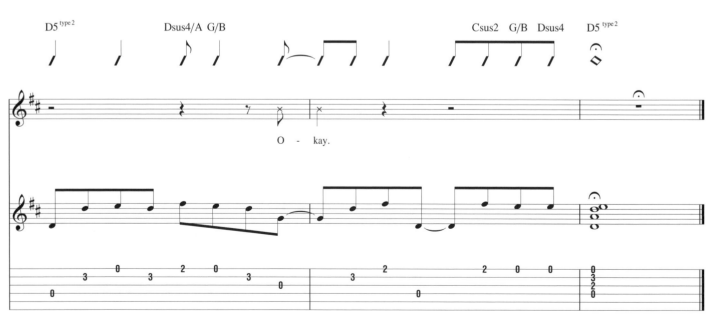

O - kay.

Ammunition

Words and Music by Jonathan Foreman

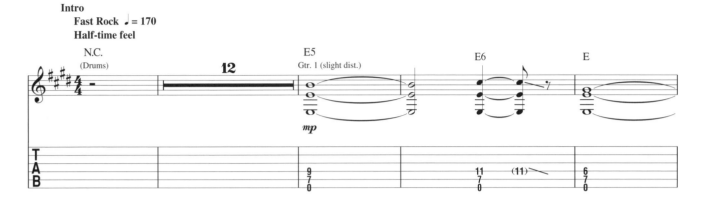

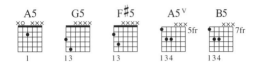

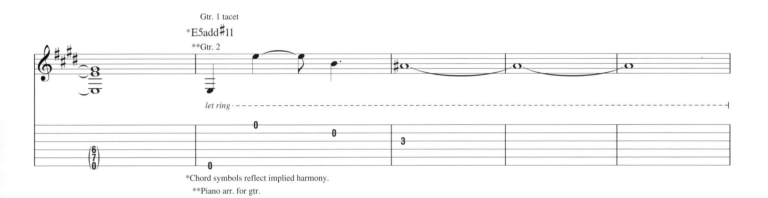

*Chord symbols reflect implied harmony.
**Piano arr. for gtr.

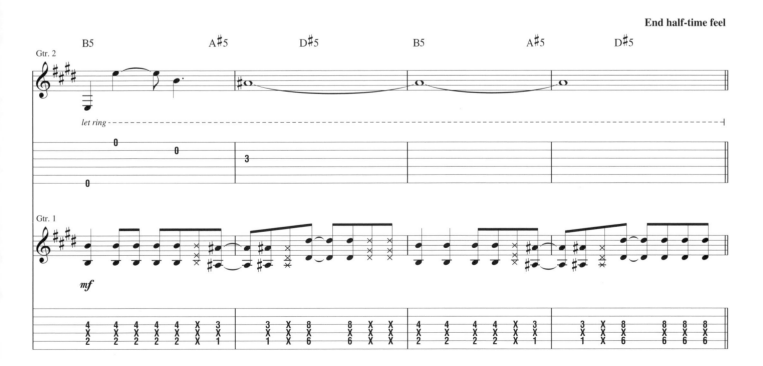

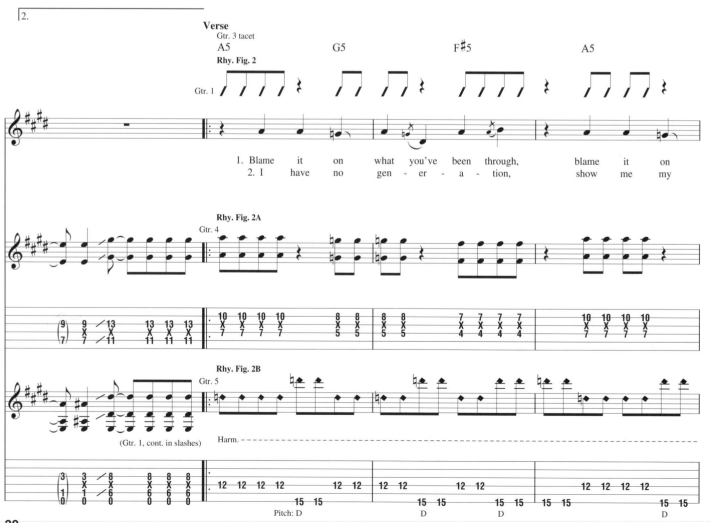

We've been blow-ing up, we're ____ the is - sue. ____ We're am - mu - ni - tion. ____

(1st time, Gtr. 6, cont. in slashes)

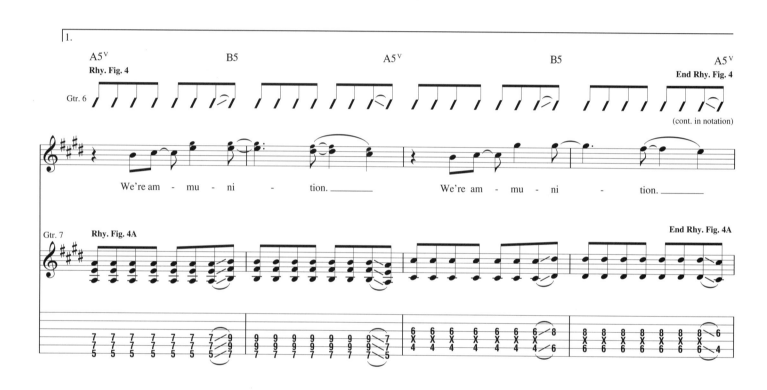

1.

We're am - mu - ni - tion. _____ We're am - mu - ni - tion. _____

Gtr. 7

Gtrs. 1 & 3: w/ Rhy. Fig. 1
Gtrs. 4 & 5: w/ Rhy. Fig. 1A
Gtrs. 6 & 7 tacet

We are ____ the fuse ____ and the am - mu - ni - tion.

Gtrs. 6 & 7

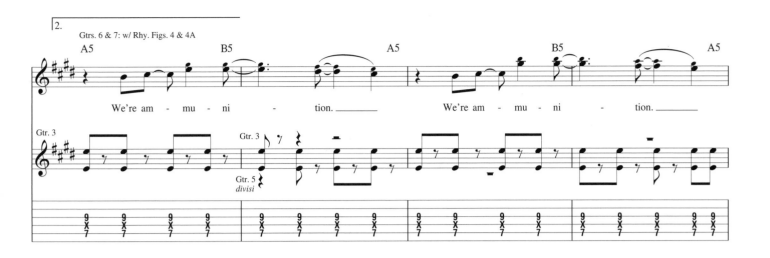

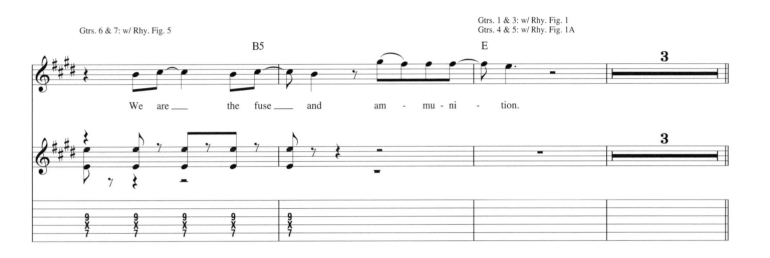

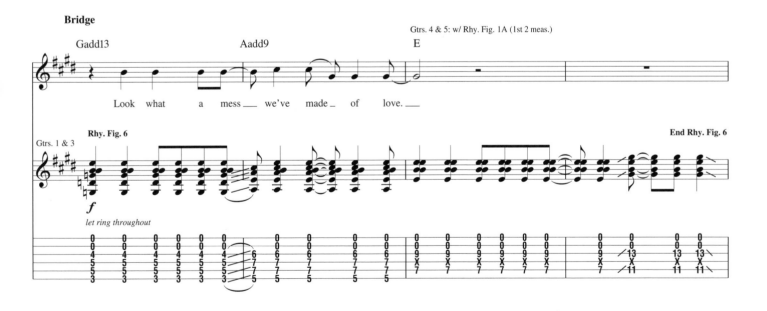

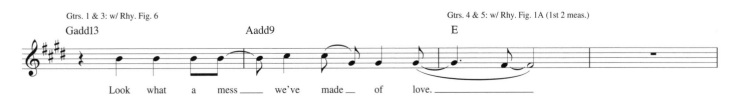

Gtrs. 1 & 3: w/ Rhy. Fig. 6 (1st 2 meas., 3 times)

Gadd13   Aadd9   Gadd13   Aadd9   Gadd13

Look what a mess __ we've made, __ we've got our - selves __ to blame. __ Look what a bomb __

Gtrs. 1 & 3: w/ Rhy. Fig. 1
Gtrs. 4 & 5: w/ Rhy. Fig. 1A

Aadd9   E

__ we've made __ of love. __

Gtr. 8 (dist.)

mp

Outro-Chorus

Gtr. 6: w/ Rhy. Fig. 3 (3 times)
Gtr. 8 tacet

B5 C#5   B5 C#5 A5   E5   F#5

We've been blow - ing up, we're __ the is - sue. __ It's our __ con - di - tion. __

Gtr. 7: w/ Rhy. Fig. 3 (2 times)

B5 C#5   B5 C#5 A5   E5   F#5

We've been blow - ing up, we're __ the is - sue, __ our det - o - na - tion, __ oh.

B5 C#5   B5 C#5 A5   E5   F#5

We've been blow - ing up, we're __ the is - sue. __ We're am - mu - ni - tion. __

Gtrs. 6 & 7: w/ Rhy. Figs. 4 & 4A

A5   B5   A5   B5   A5

We're am - mu - ni - tion. __ We're am - mu - ni - tion. __

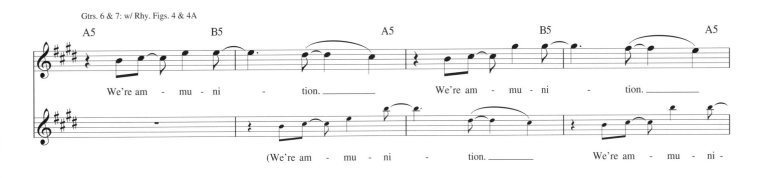

Dare You to Move

Words and Music by Jonathan Foreman

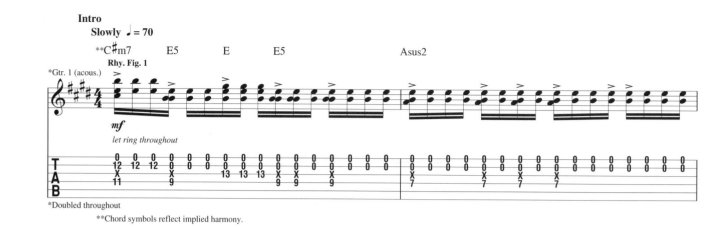

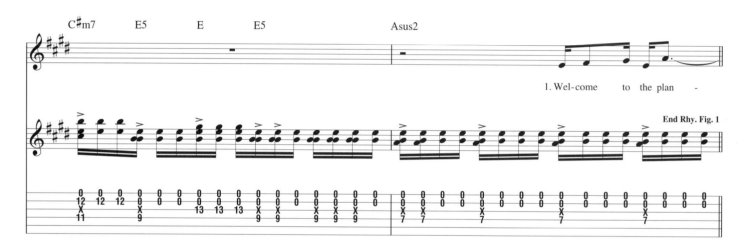

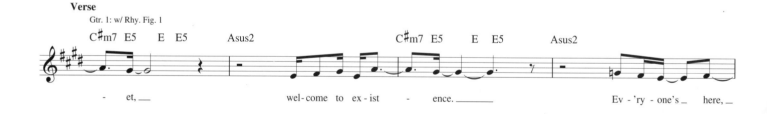

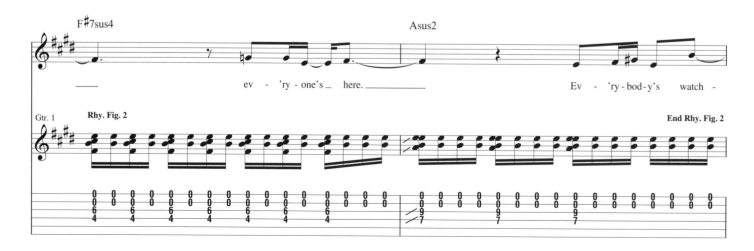

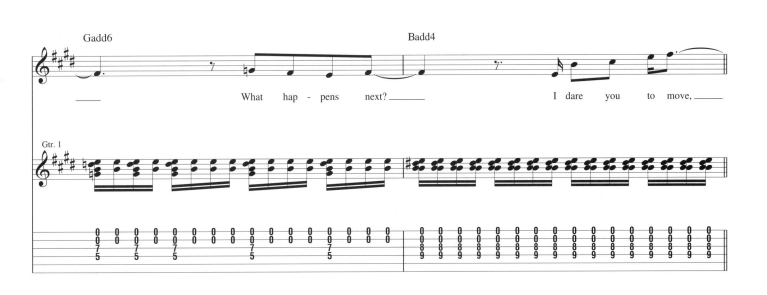

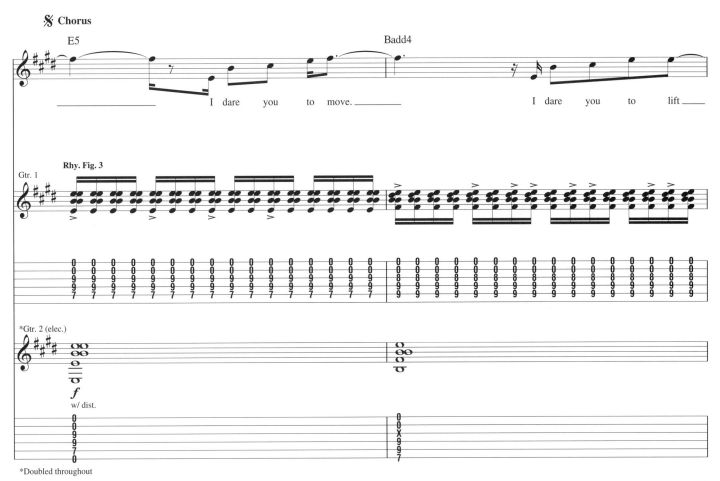

*Doubled throughout

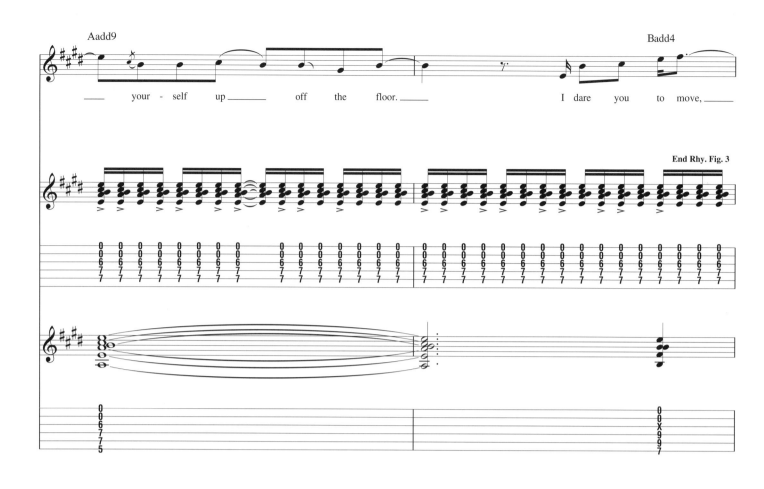

your - self up _____ off the floor. _____   I dare you to move, _____

End Rhy. Fig. 3

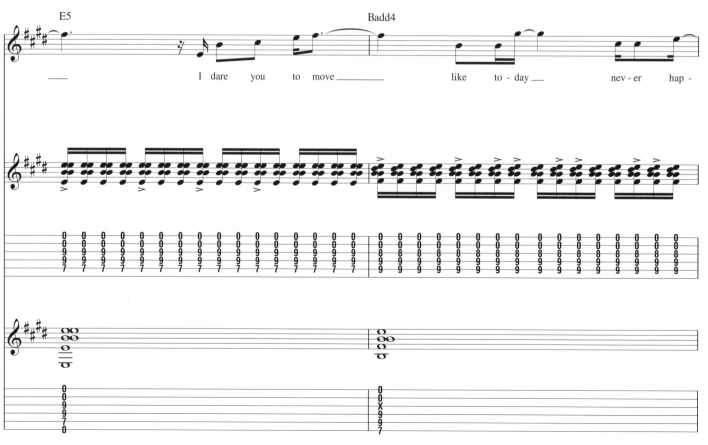

I dare you to move _____ like to - day _____ nev - er hap -

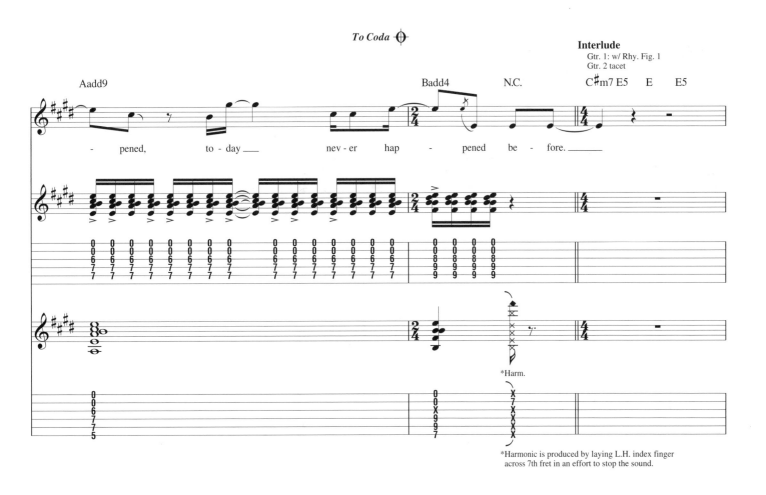

*Harmonic is produced by laying L.H. index finger
across 7th fret in an effort to stop the sound.

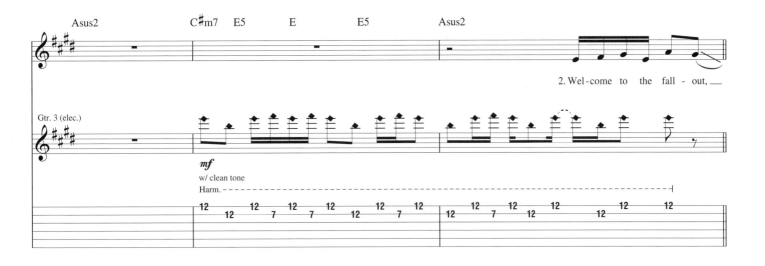

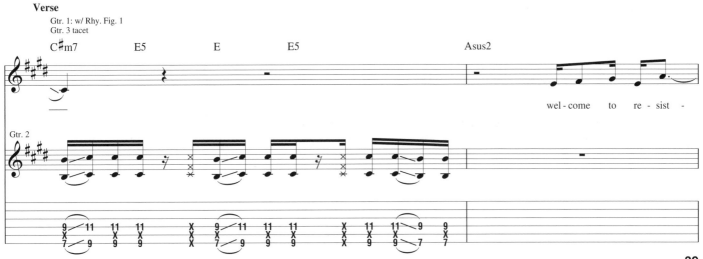

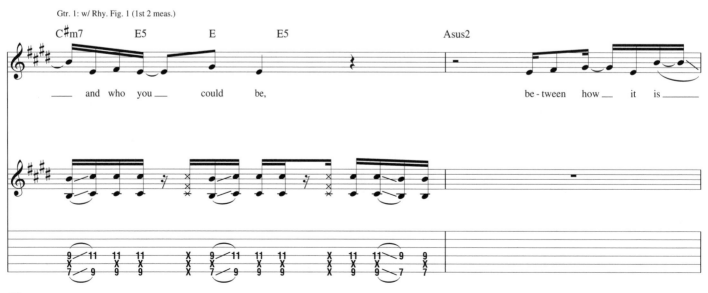

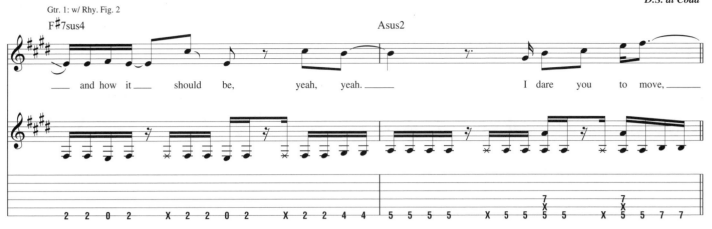

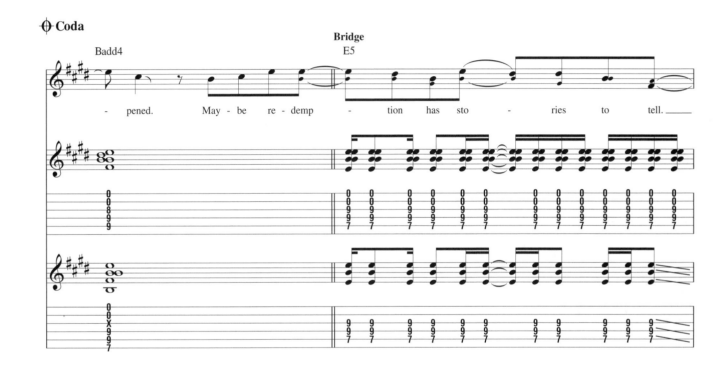

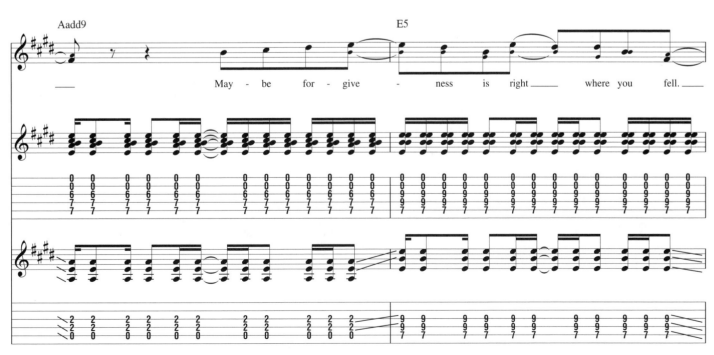

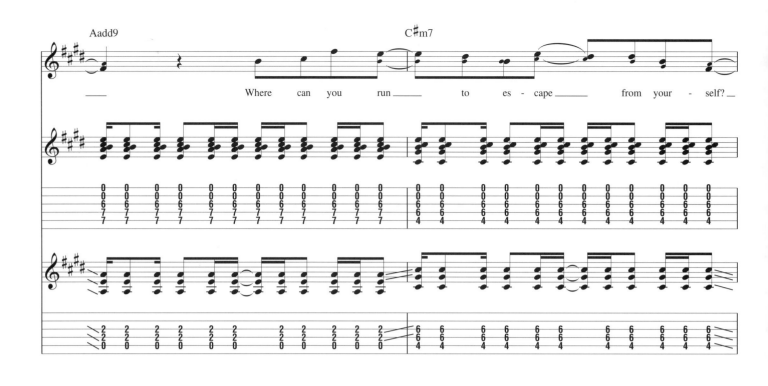

Where can you run ___ to es-cape ___ from your-self? ___

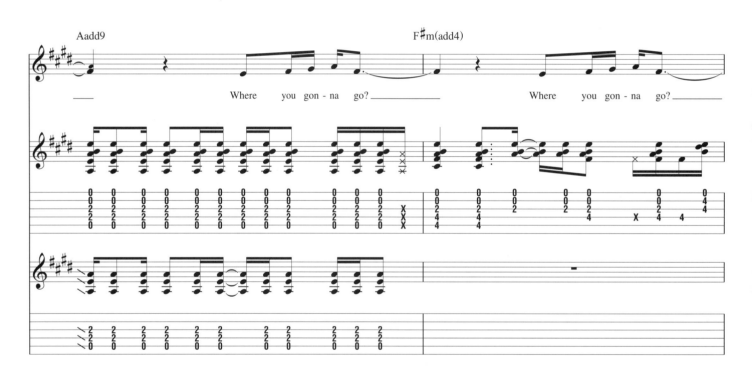

Where you gon-na go? ___ Where you gon-na go? ___

Interlude
Gtrs. 1 & 2 tacet

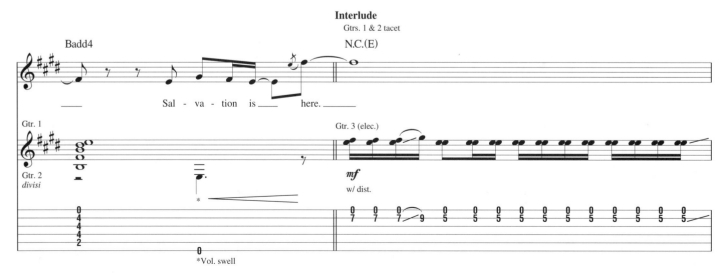

Sal - va - tion is ___ here. ___

Gtr. 1

Gtr. 2
divisi

Gtr. 3 (elec.)

mf
w/ dist.

*Vol. swell

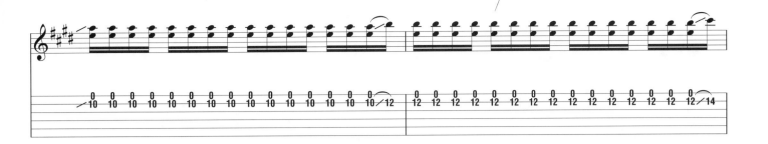

Outro-Chorus
Gtr. 1: w/ Rhy. Fig. 3 (1 1/2 times)
Gtr. 3 tacet

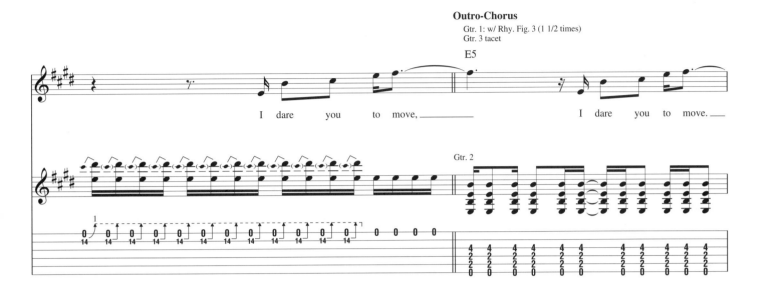

I dare you to move, _____ I dare you to move. _____

Gtr. 2

_____ I dare you to lift _____ your-self, _____ lift your-self up off the

floor. _____ I dare _____ you to move, _____ I dare _____ you to _____ move _____

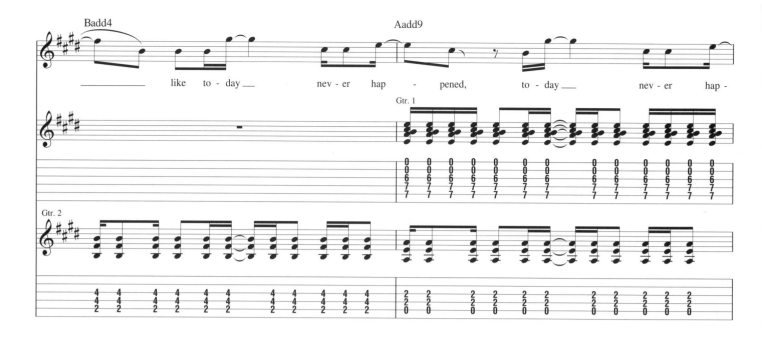

like to - day ___ nev - er hap - pened, to - day ___ nev - er hap -

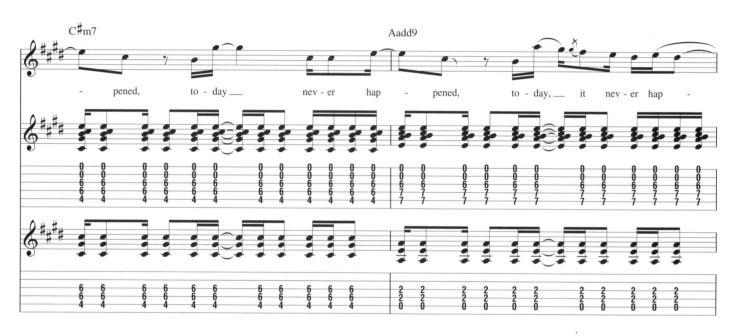

- pened, to - day ___ nev - er hap - pened, to - day, ___ it nev - er hap -

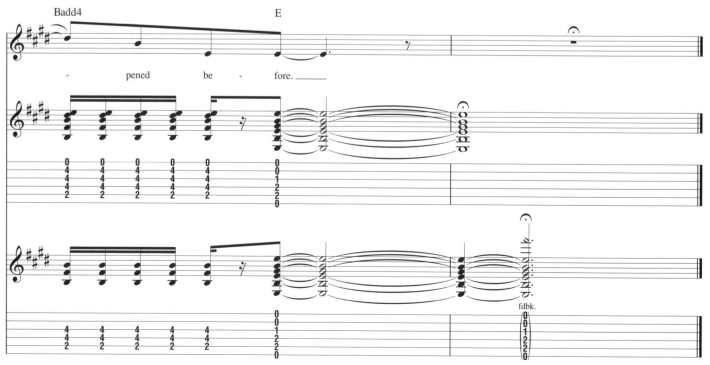

- pened be - fore. ___

Redemption

Words and Music by Jonathan Foreman

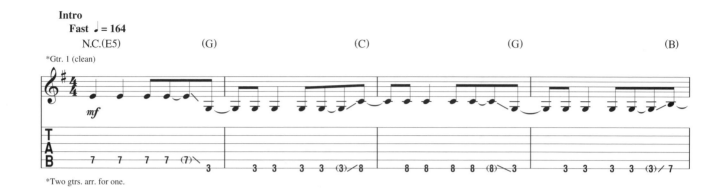

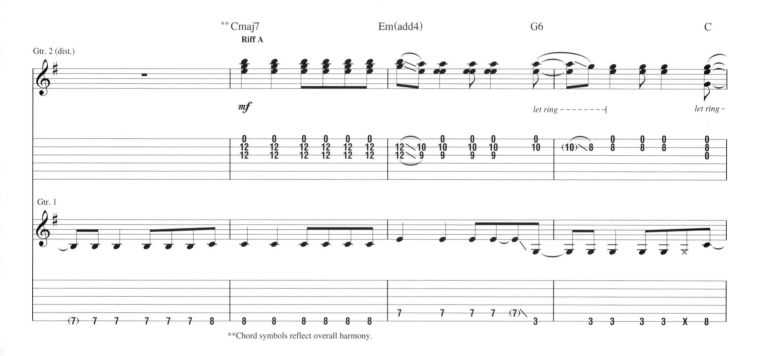

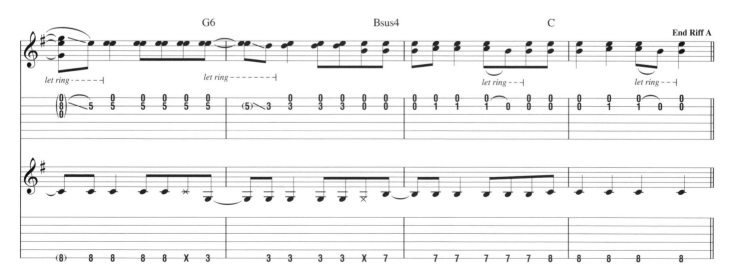

Verse

Gtr. 2 tacet

1. Four A. M., two hours to go, I'm wear-ing out a lone-

Gtr. 1

*Doubled throughout

-ly glow. I miss you more than I can know.

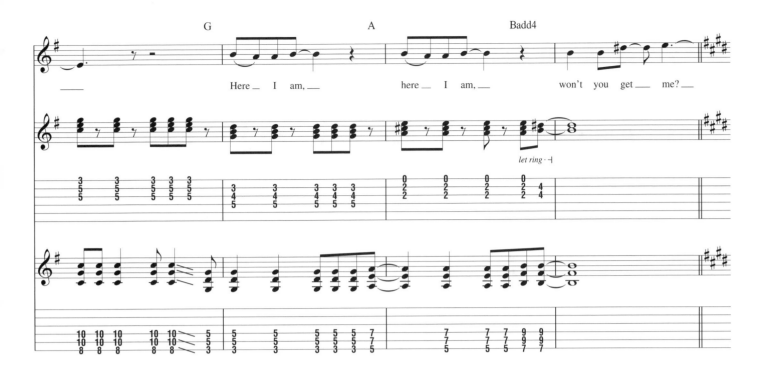

Here __ I am, __ here __ I am, __ won't you get __ me? __

let ring

§ Chorus

2nd & 3rd times, Gtr. 3: w/ Rhy. Fill 1

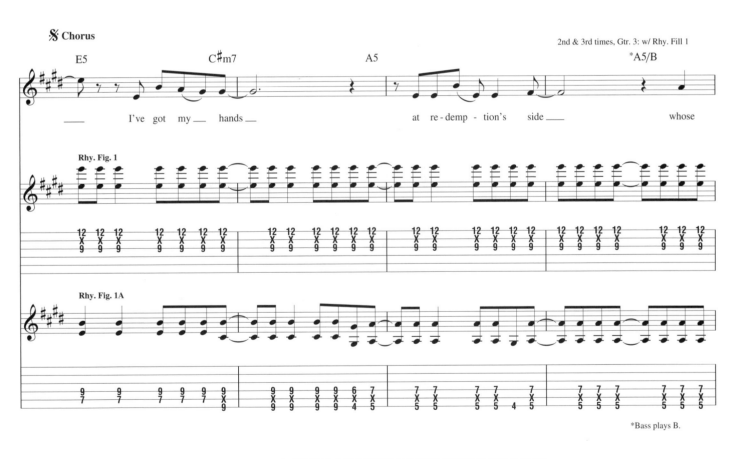

I've got my __ hands __ at re-demp-tion's side __ whose

Rhy. Fig. 1

Rhy. Fig. 1A

*Bass plays B.

Rhy. Fill 1
Gtr. 3

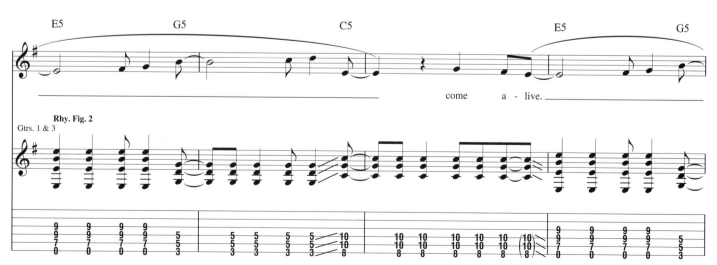

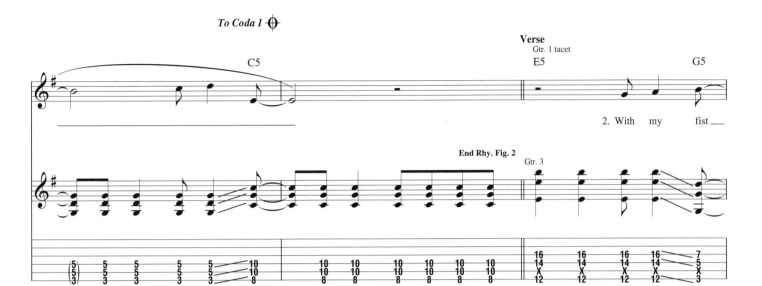

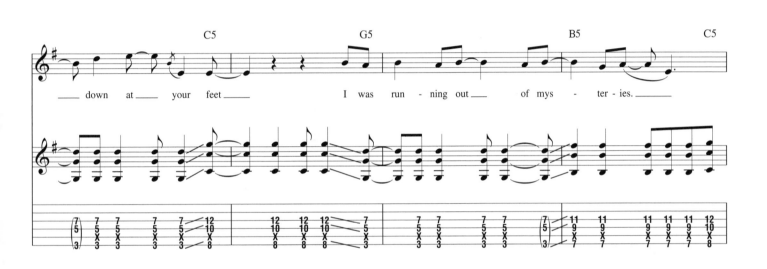

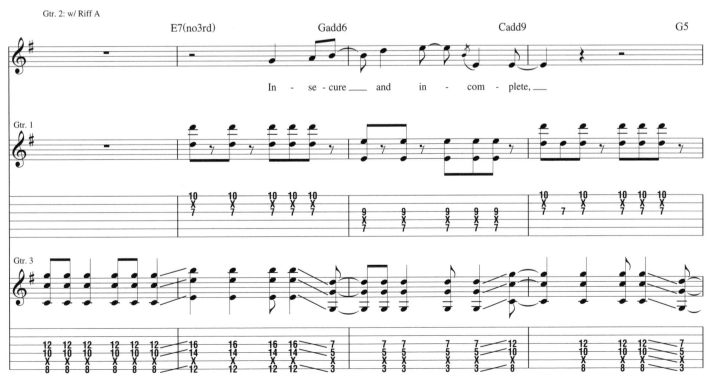

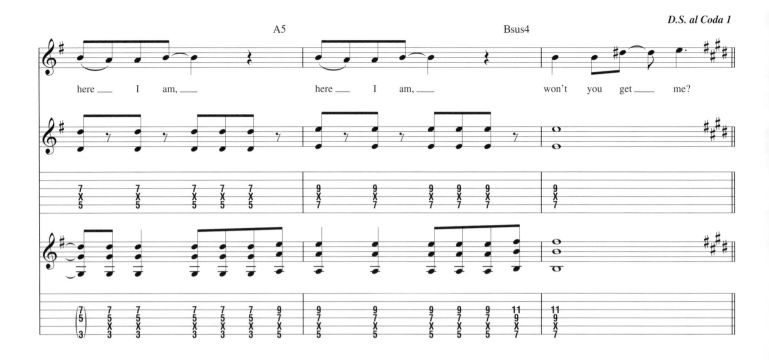

♦ **Coda 1**

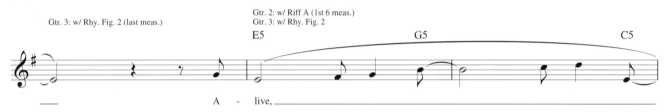

Bridge

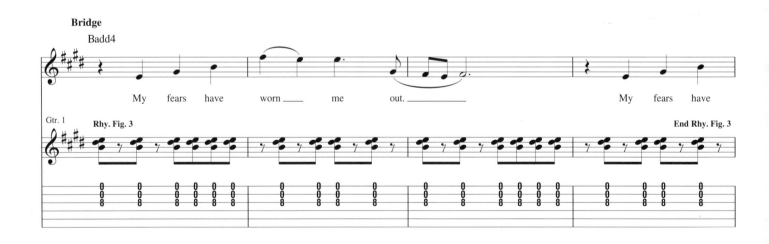

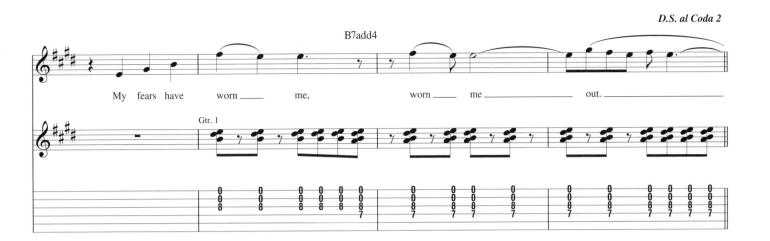

My fears have worn ____ me, worn ____ me _____ out. _____

⊕ Coda 2

and I'll come ____ a - live, _____   at re-demp - tion's side. ____ whose
(Got my ____ hands, _____)

scars,   Big - ger than, ____ these doubts of mine. ____ I'll fit all of these ____ mon -
big - ger than.) ____

stros - i - ties ____ in - side _____   and come a - live, _____

____ come a - live. _____

The Beautiful Letdown

Words and Music by Jonathan Foreman

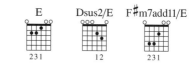

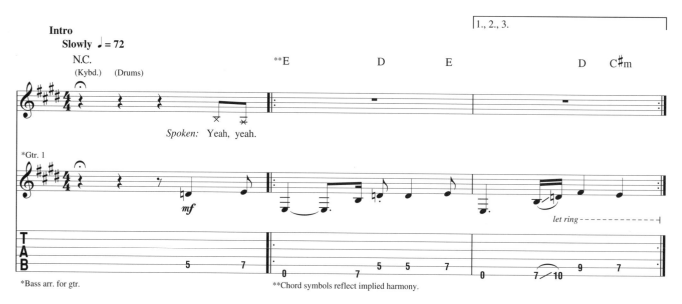

*Bass arr. for gtr.

**Chord symbols reflect implied harmony.

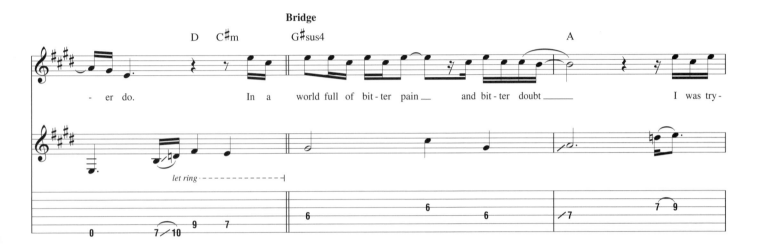

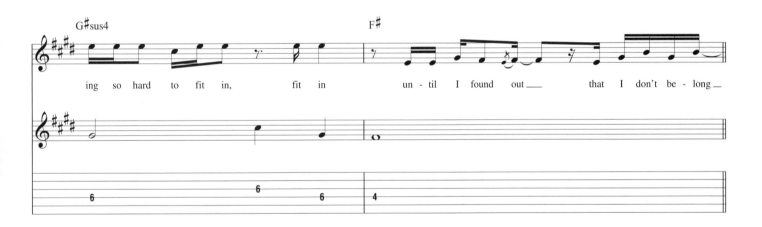

53

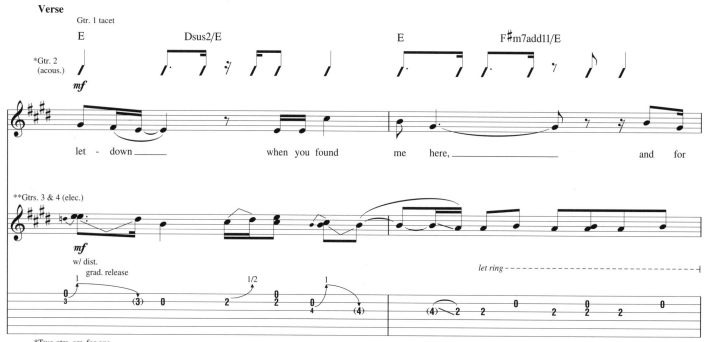

*Two gtrs. arr. for one.
**Composite arrangement

once in a rare blue moon ___ I see ev - 'ry - thing clear. I'll be a beau - ti - ful

let - down, ___ that's what I'll for - ev - er be, ___ and

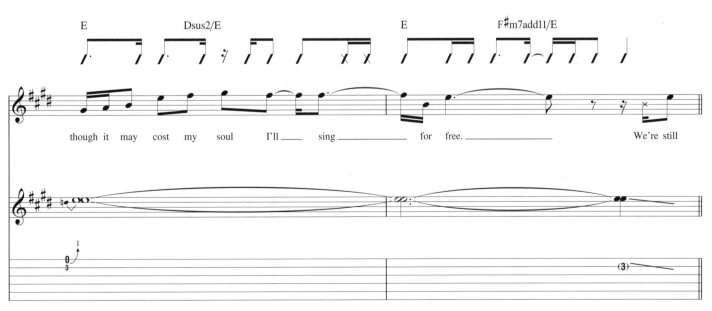

though it may cost my soul I'll ___ sing ___ for free. ___ We're still

Bridge

chas-ing our tails ___ and the ris - ing ___ sun, ___ and our

(Yeah, yeah, yeah, yeah, yeah. Ba, da, ba, da, da.

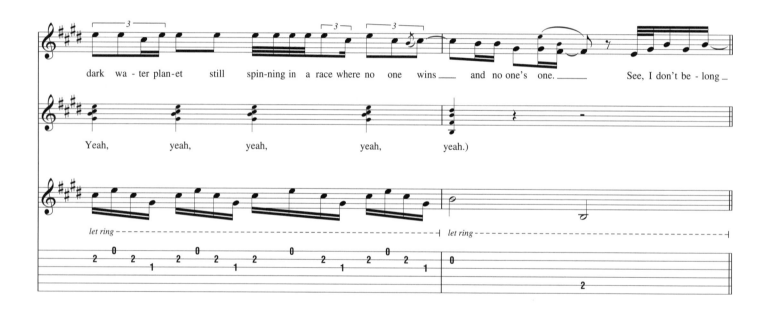

dark wa - ter plan-et still spin-ning in a race where no one wins ___ and no one's one. ___ See, I don't be - long ___

Yeah, yeah, yeah, yeah, yeah.)

Chorus

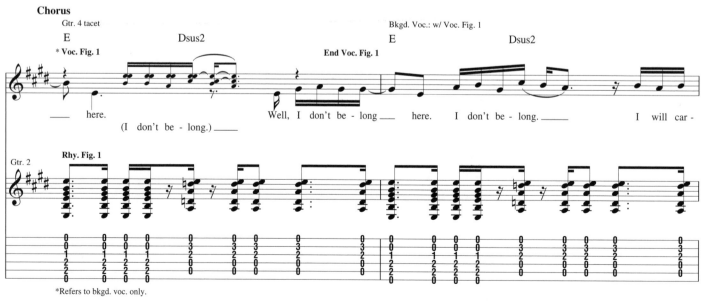

___ here. Well, I don't be - long ___ here. I don't be - long. ___ I will car -

(I don't be - long.) ___

*Refers to bkgd. voc. only.

56

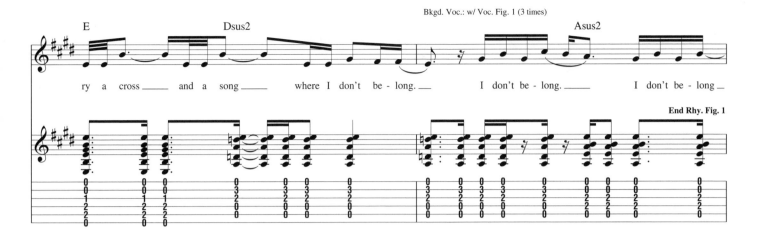

ry a cross _____ and a song _____ where I don't be - long. _____ I don't be - long. _____ I don't be - long _

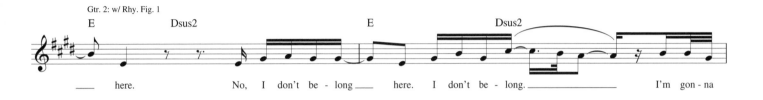

_____ here. No, I don't be - long _____ here. I don't be - long. _____ I'm gon - na

set sight _ and set sail _ for the king-dom come, _ king-dom come, _ Your king - dom come. _ Won't you let _ me

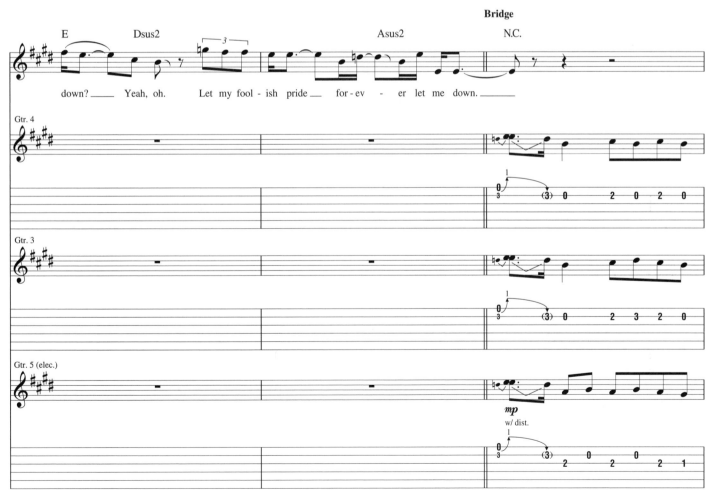

down? _____ Yeah, oh. Let my fool - ish pride _____ for - ev - er let me down. _____

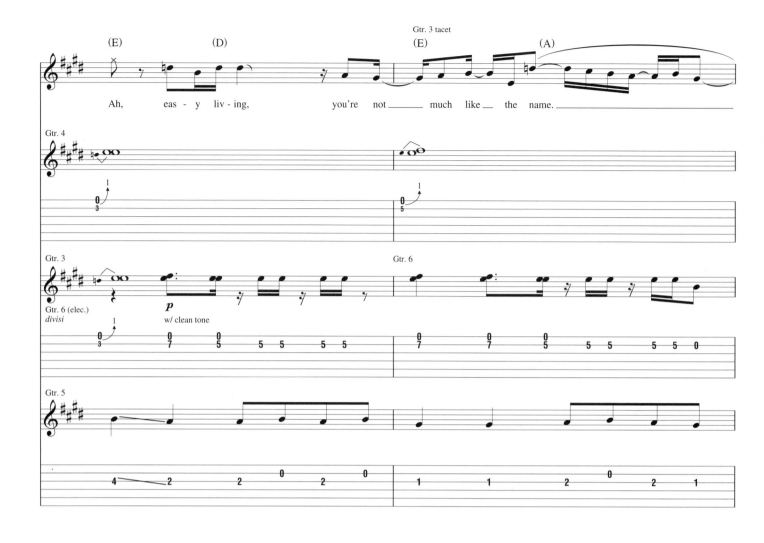

Ah, eas - y liv - ing, you're not _____ much like _____ the name. _____

_____ Eas - y dy - ing, hey, _____ you look just a - bout _____ the same. _____ Would you please _____

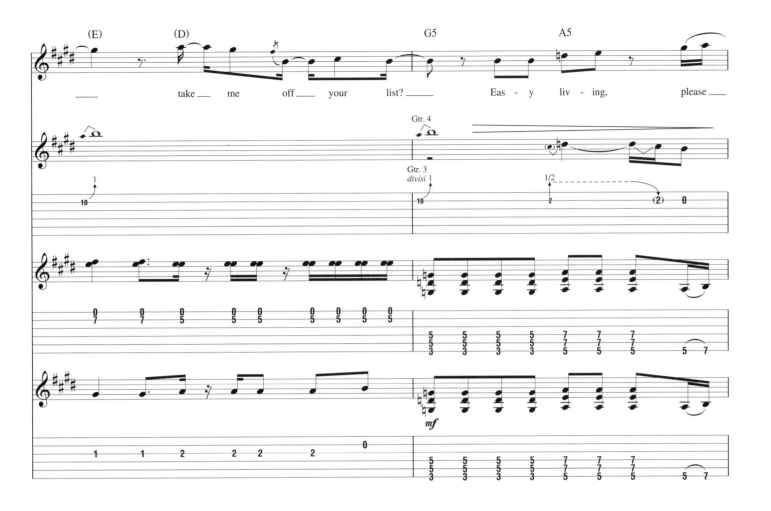

take __ me off __ your list? ___ Eas - y liv - ing, please ___

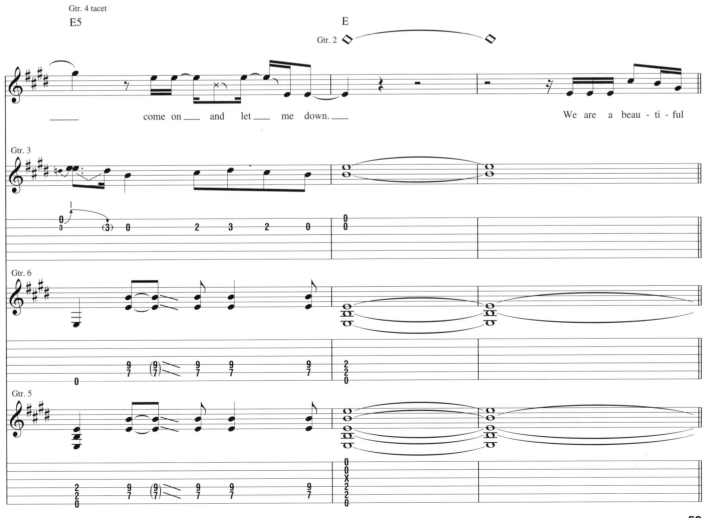

Gtr. 4 tacet

E5

come on __ and let __ me down. ___

E

We are a beau - ti - ful

Pre-Chorus

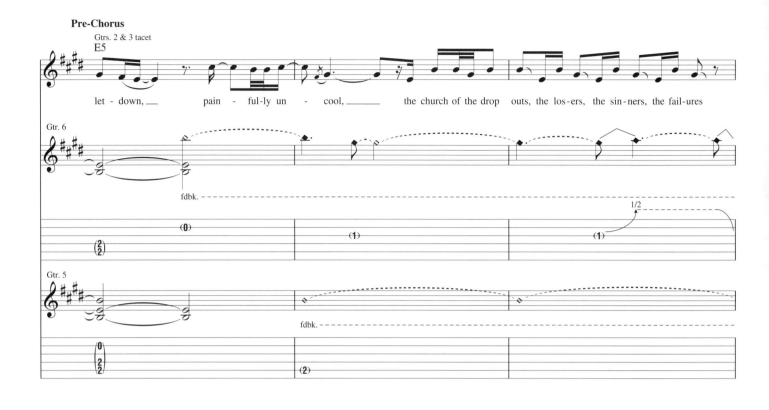

let - down, ___ pain - ful - ly un - cool, ___ the church of the drop outs, the los-ers, the sin-ners, the fail-ures

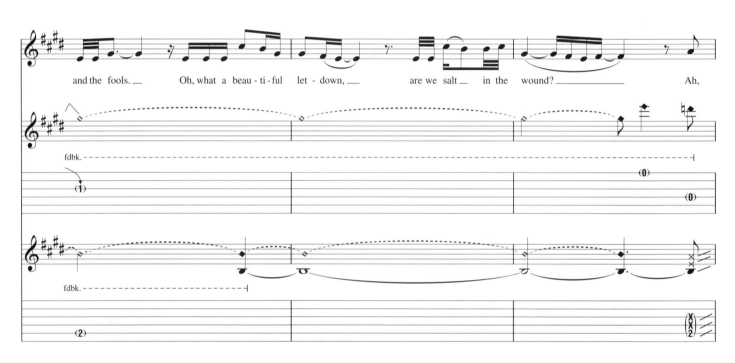

and the fools. ___ Oh, what a beau-ti-ful let - down, ___ are we salt ___ in the wound? ___ Ah,

Chorus

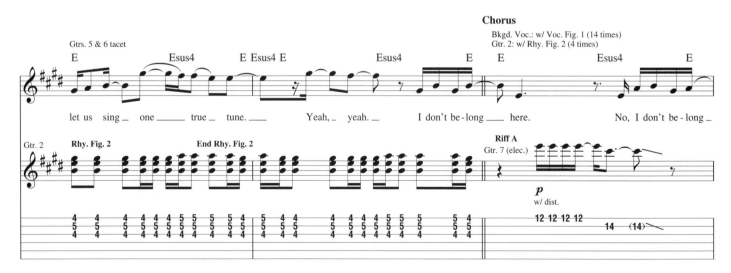

let us sing ___ one ___ true ___ tune. ___ Yeah, ___ yeah. ___ I don't be-long ___ here. No, I don't be-long ___

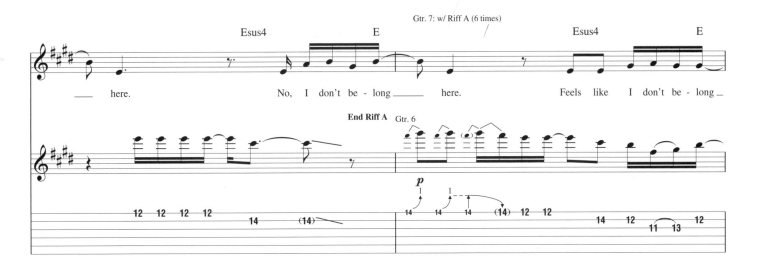

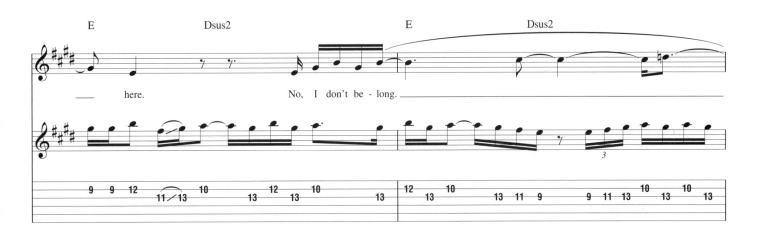

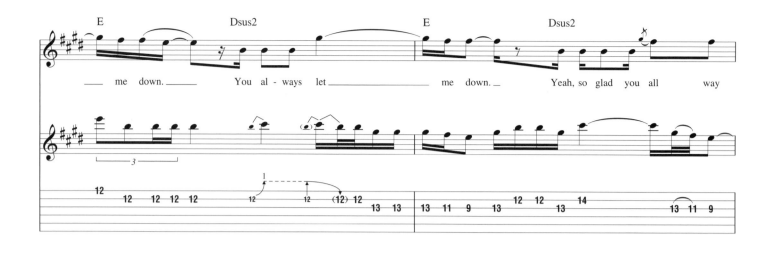

___ me down. ___ You al - ways let _____ me down. __ Yeah, so glad you all way

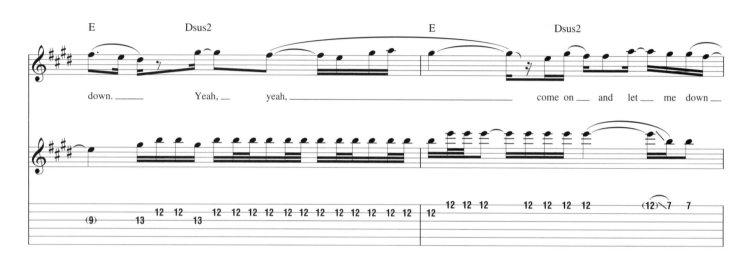

down. _____ Yeah, __ yeah, _____ come on __ and let __ me down __

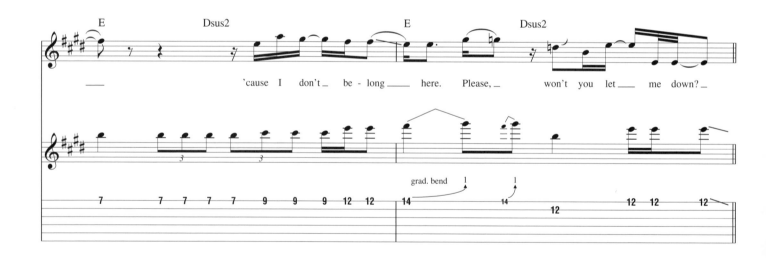

___ 'cause I don't _ be - long ___ here. Please, _ won't you let __ me down? _

Fade out

Outro

Gtr. 6 tacet   Gtr. 2 tacet

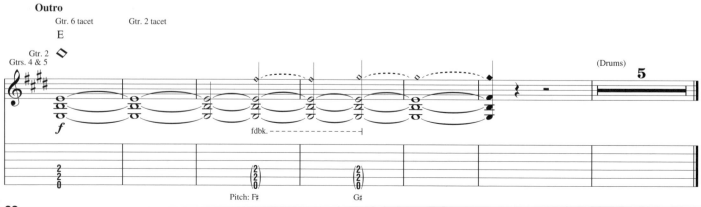

Gone

Words and Music by Jonathan Foreman and Tim Foreman

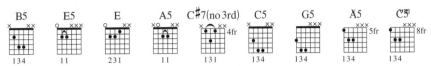

- up than try and fix what's go - in' on, ____ but the prob - lem keeps on

call - ing e - ven with the cell ____ phone gone. She told him ____ that she be - lieves in

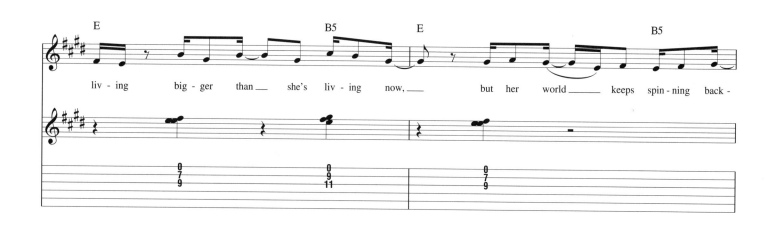

liv - ing big - ger than ____ she's liv - ing now, ____ but her world _____ keeps spin - ning back -

Pre-Chorus

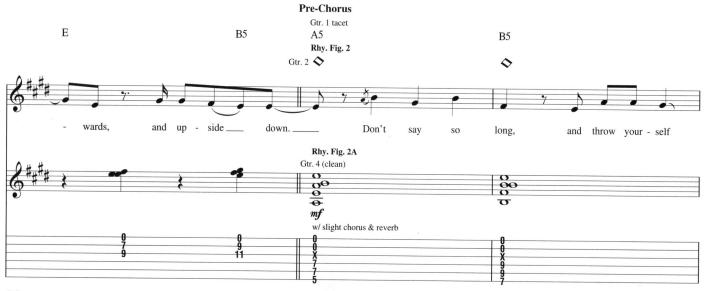

- wards, and up - side ____ down. ____ Don't say so long, and throw your - self

64

long, you're not that far gone. This could be __ your big chance to make __ up. To - day will soon __ be

Chorus

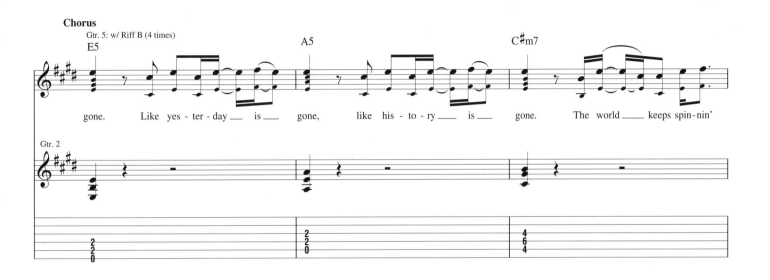

gone. Like yes - ter - day __ is __ gone, like his - to - ry __ is __ gone. The world __ keeps spin - nin'

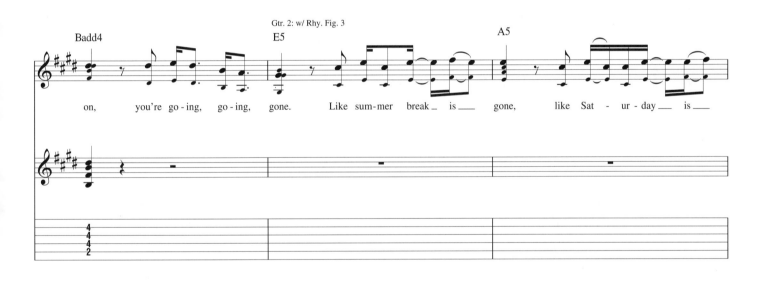

on, you're go - ing, go - ing, gone. Like sum - mer break __ is __ gone, like Sat - ur - day __ is __

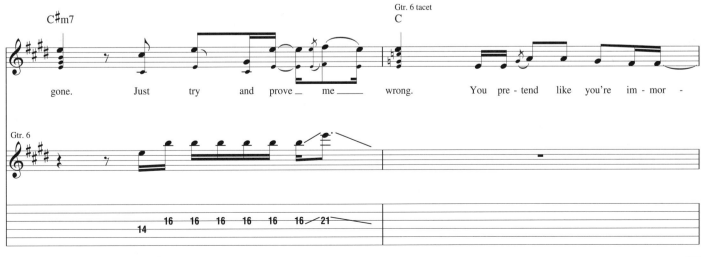

gone. Just try and prove __ me __ wrong. You pre - tend like you're im - mor -

67

Gtr. 1: w/ Riff A (1st 2 meas.)

-tal.
(You're im-mor -tal,   You're im-mor -tal,   ha, ha.
                                                  you're im-mor -tal.)

Gtr. 2

(cont. in slashes)

Bridge

Rhy. Fig. 4

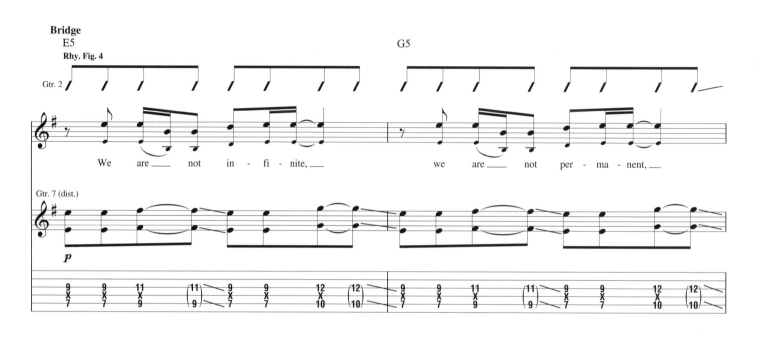

Gtr. 2

We are ___ not in - fi - nite, ___   we are ___ not per - ma - nent, ___

Gtr. 7 (dist.)

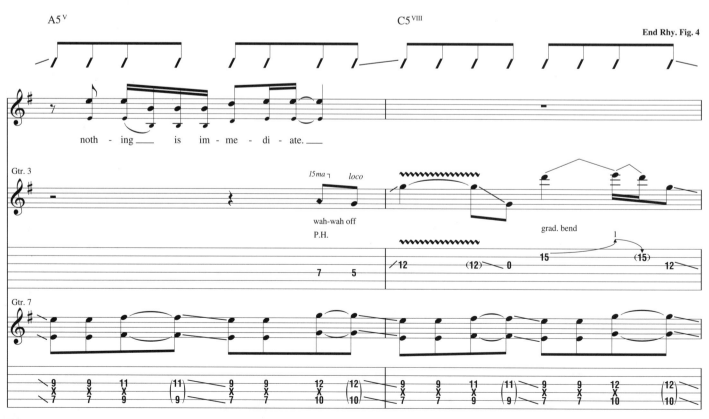

End Rhy. Fig. 4

noth - ing ___ is im - me - di - ate. ___

Gtr. 3

15ma⌐ loco

wah-wah off
P.H.

grad. bend

Gtr. 7

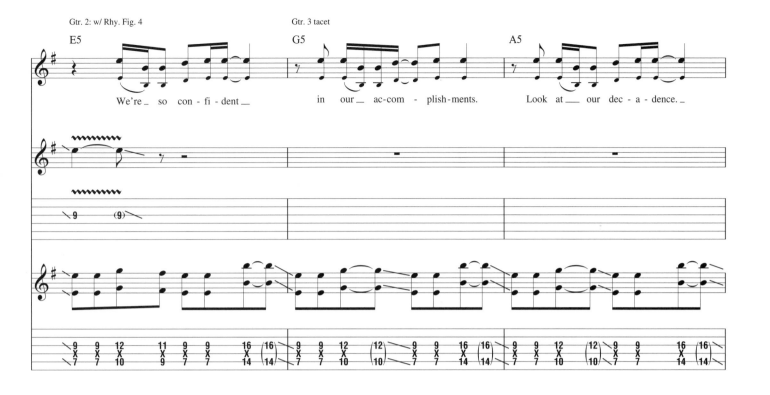

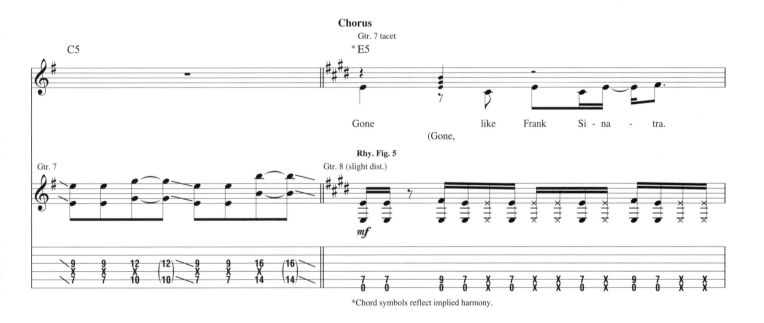

*Chord symbols reflect implied harmony.

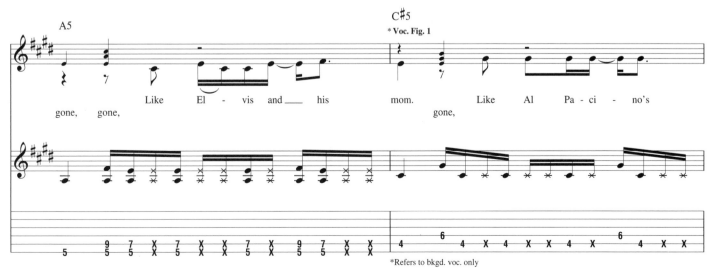

*Refers to bkgd. voc. only

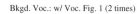

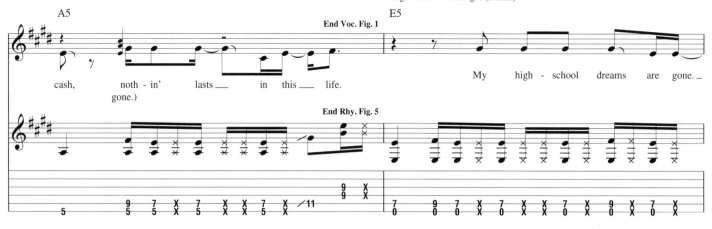

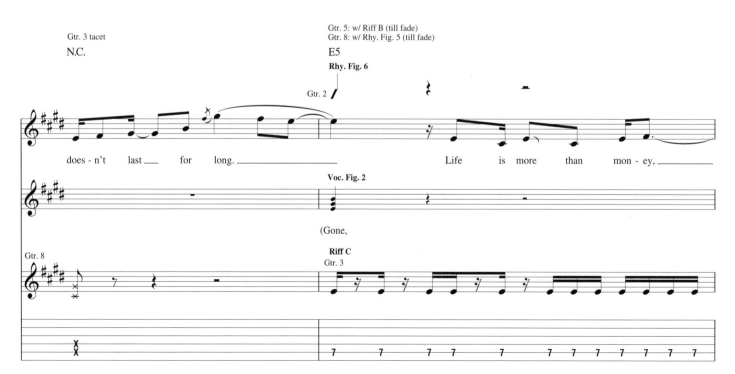

70

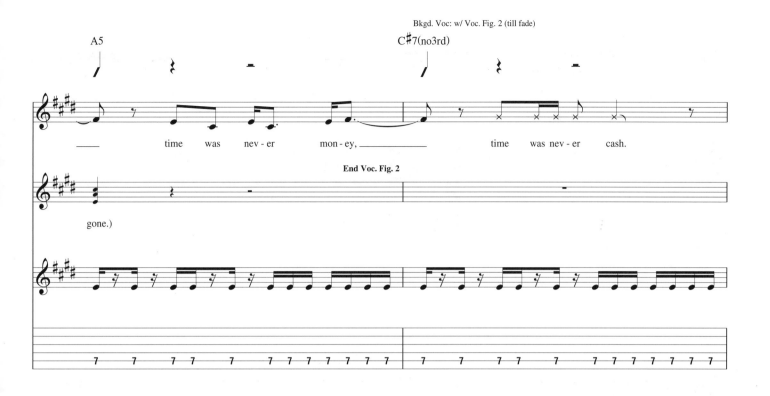

time was nev-er mon-ey, _____ time was nev-er cash.

gone.)

Life is still __ more than girls. _ Life is more _ than hun-dred dol-lar bills __ and

ro-to-tom __ fills. Life is more than fame and rock __ and roll ____ and thrills.

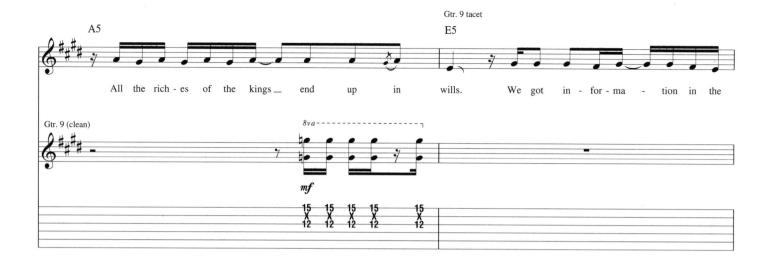

All the rich-es of the kings __ end up in wills. We got in - for-ma - tion in the

in - for-ma - tion age, __ but do we know __ what life is out - side of our __

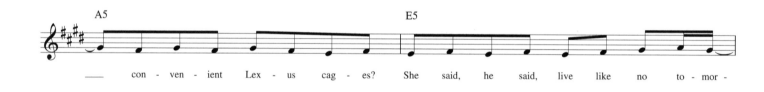

__ con - ven - ient Lex - us cag - es? She said, he said, live like no to - mor -

- row, ev - 'ry mo - ment that we bor - row brings us clos - er to the God __

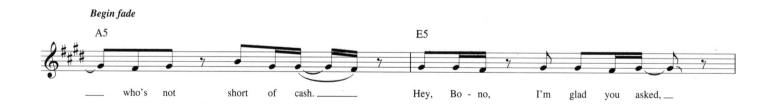

__ who's not short of cash. __ Hey, Bo - no, I'm glad you asked, __

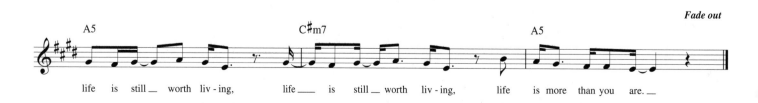

life is still __ worth liv - ing, life __ is still __ worth liv - ing, life is more than you are. __

On Fire

Words and Music by Jonathan Foreman and Daniel Victor

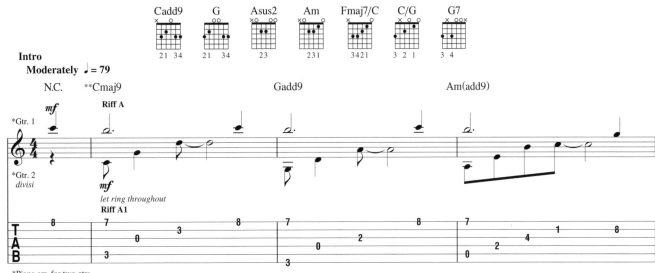

*Piano arr. for two gtrs.

**Chord symbols reflect implied harmony.

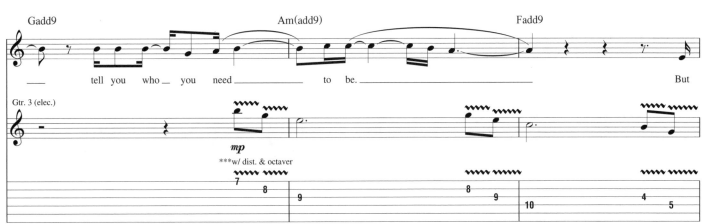

***Set octaver for one octave above.

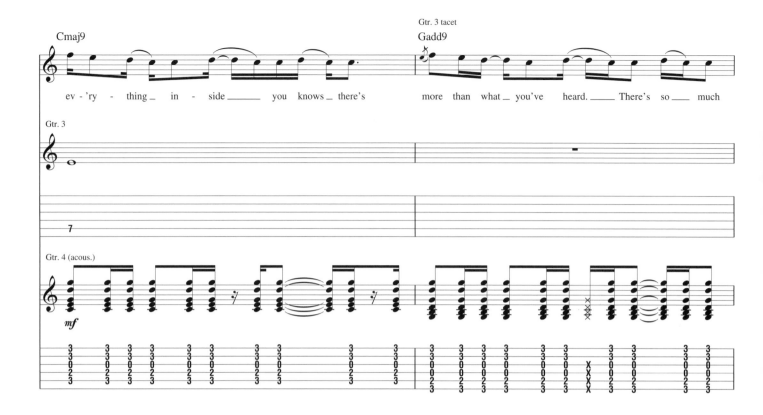

ev - 'ry - thing_ in - side _____ you knows _ there's more than what _ you've heard. _____ There's so _ much

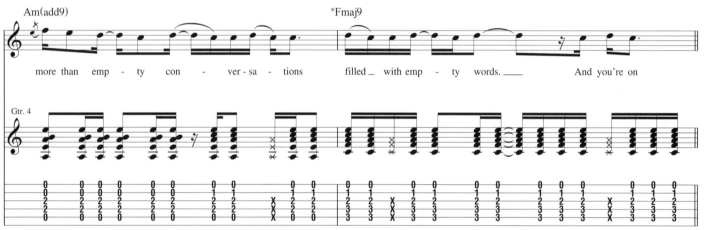

more than emp - ty con - ver - sa - tions filled _ with emp - ty words. _____ And you're on

*Chord symbols reflect overall harmony.

Chorus

Gtrs. 1 & 2: w/ Riffs A & A1

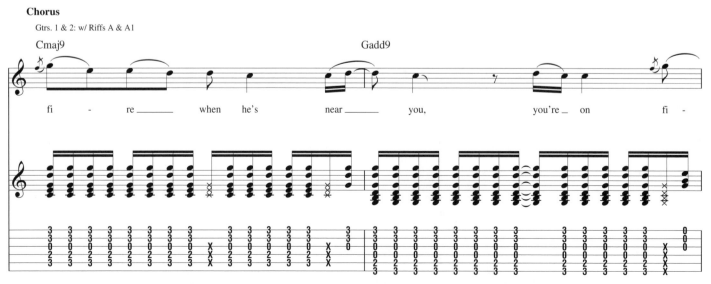

fi - re _____ when he's near _____ you, you're _ on fi -

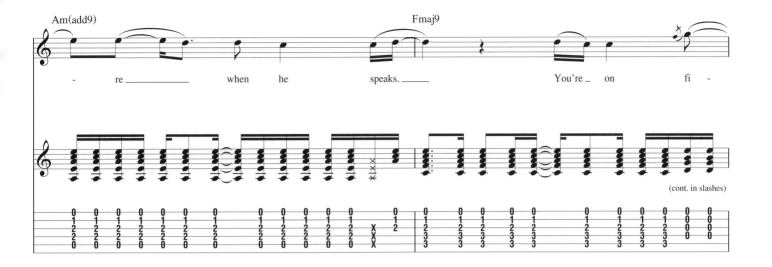

-re _____ when he speaks. _____ You're_ on fi-

(cont. in slashes)

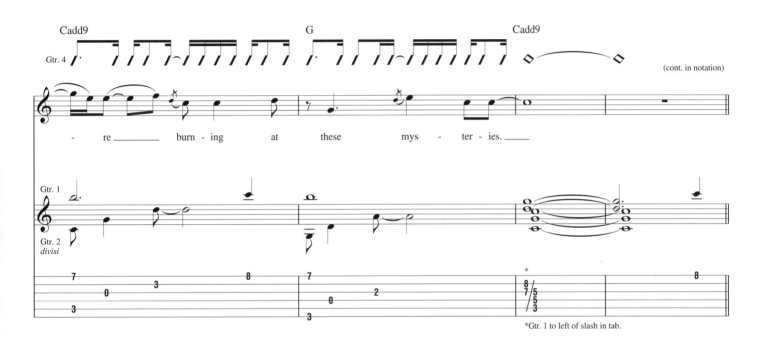

-re _____ burn-ing at these mys - ter - ies. _____

(cont. in notation)

*Gtr. 1 to left of slash in tab.

Verse

Gtrs. 1 & 2: w/ Riffs A & A1 (3 times)

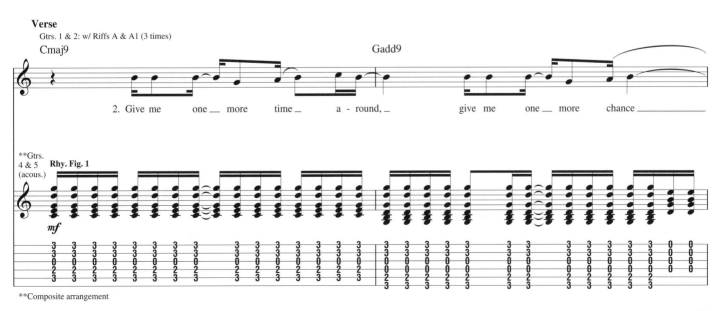

2. Give me one _ more time _ a - round, _ give me one _ more chance _____

**Gtrs. 4 & 5 (acous.) **Rhy. Fig. 1

mf

**Composite arrangement

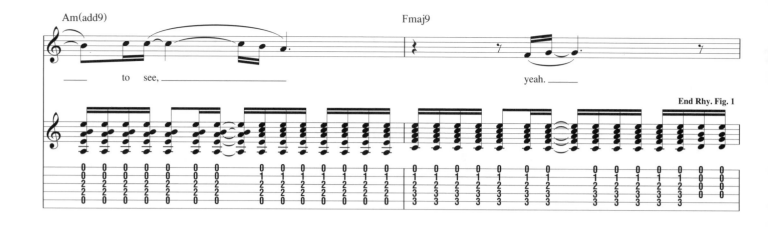

Am(add9) ... to see, ... yeah. Fmaj9

End Rhy. Fig. 1

Gtrs. 4 & 5: w/ Rhy. Fig. 1 (2 times)

Cmaj9   Gadd9   Am(add9)

Give me ev-'ry-thing you are, give me one more chance to be near you, yeah,

Fmaj9   Cmaj9   Gadd9

yeah. When ev-'ry-thing in-side me looks like ev-'ry-thing I hate, you are the hope

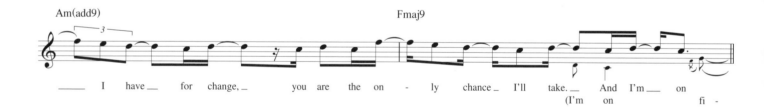

Am(add9)   Fmaj9

I have for change, you are the on-ly chance I'll take. And I'm on
(I'm on fi-

Chorus

Gtrs. 1 & 2: w/ Riffs A & A1 (1 1/2 times)
Gtrs. 4 & 5: w/ Rhy. Fig. 1 (1 1/2 times)

Cmaj9   Gadd9   Am(add9)

* **Voc. Fig. 1**

fi - re when you're near me, and I'm on fi - re when you speak.
-re, I'm on fi - re,

*Refers to bkgd. voc. only.

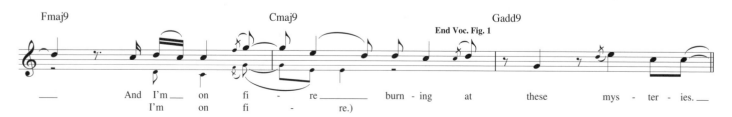

Fmaj9   Cmaj9   Gadd9

End Voc. Fig. 1

And I'm on fi - re burn-ing at these mys - ter-ies.
I'm on fi - re.)

Bridge

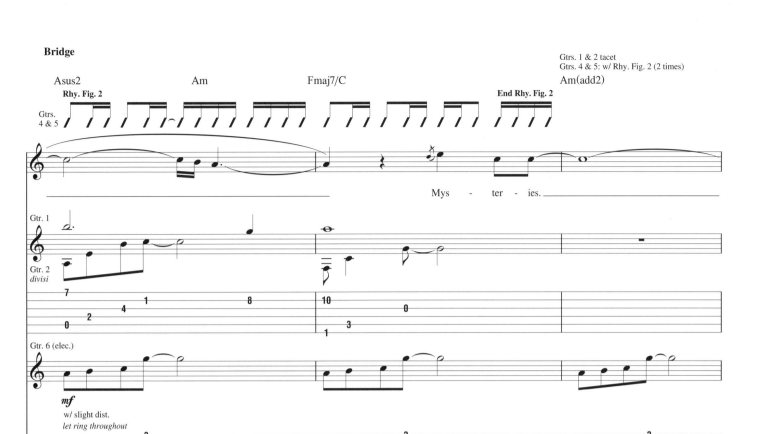

Mys - ter - ies.

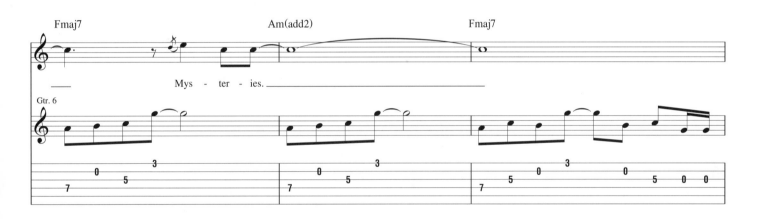

Mys - ter - ies.

Interlude

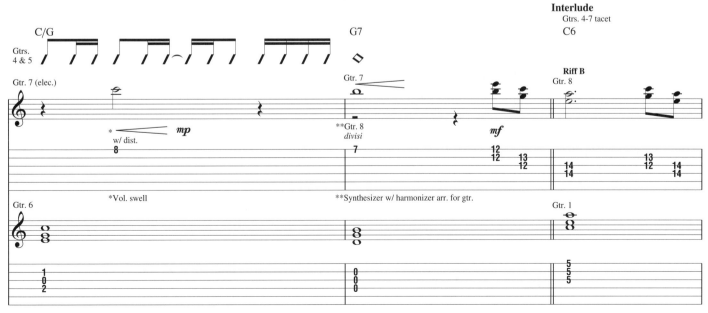

*Vol. swell

**Synthesizer w/ harmonizer arr. for gtr.

Chorus

Gtrs. 1 & 2: w/ Riffs A & A1 (7 times)
Gtrs. 4 & 5: w/ Rhy. Fig. 1 (7 times)
Gtr. 8: w/ Riff B (2 1/2 times)

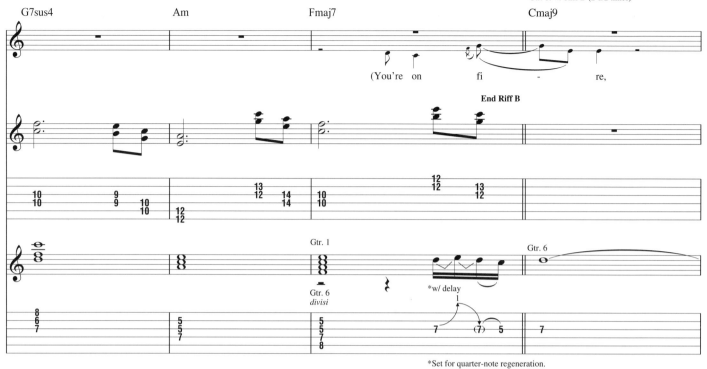

*Set for quarter-note regeneration.

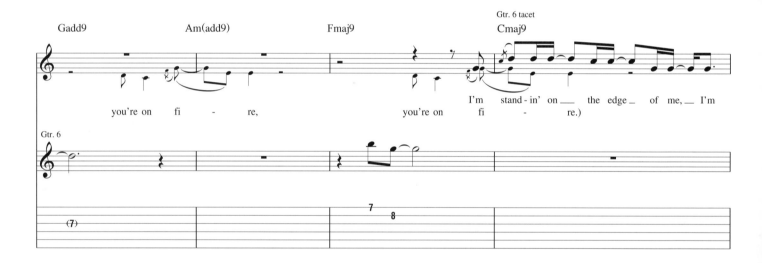

**Set delay for dotted eighth-note regeneration.

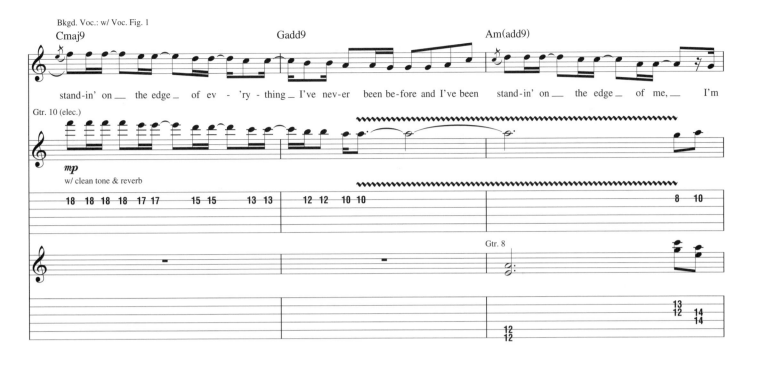

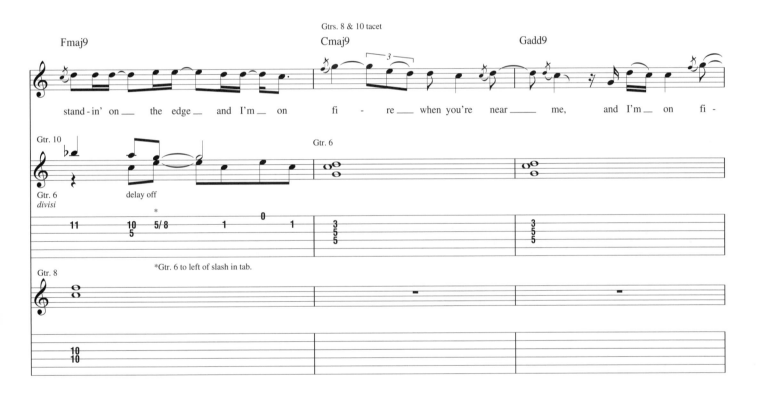

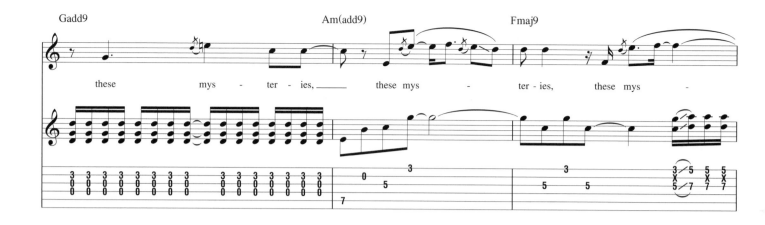

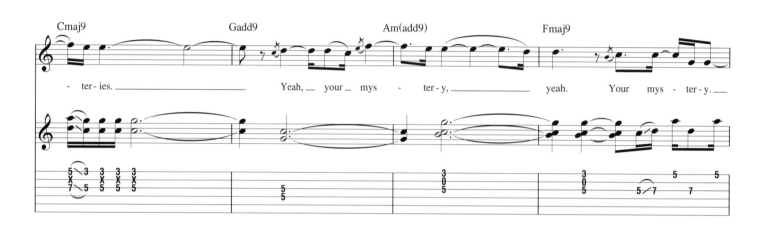

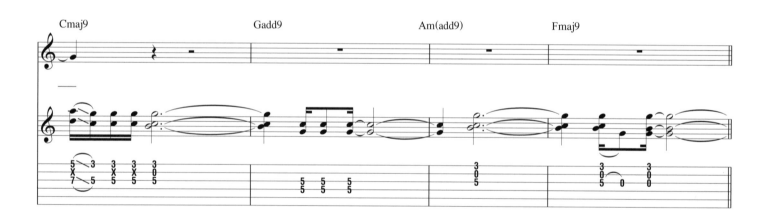

Outro

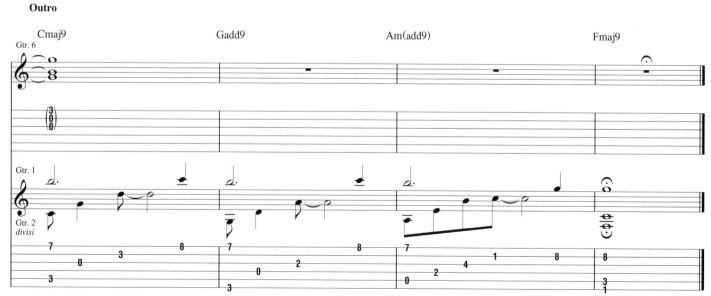

Adding to the Noise

Words and Music by Jonathan Foreman and Tim Foreman

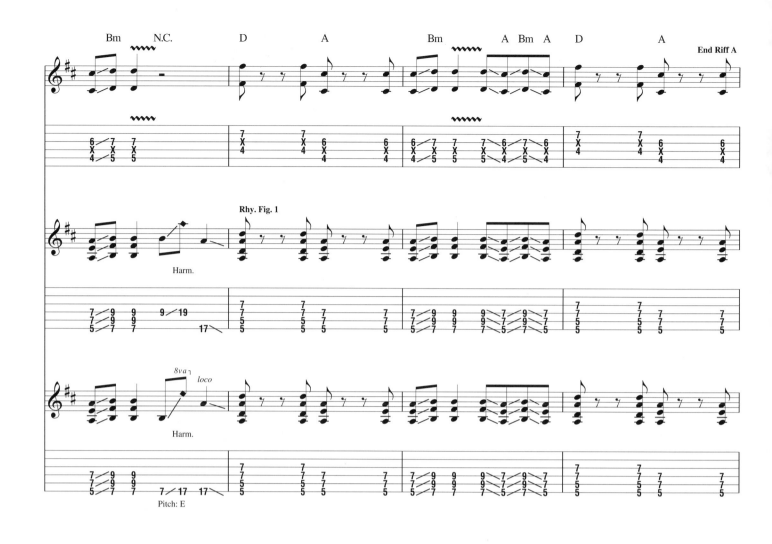

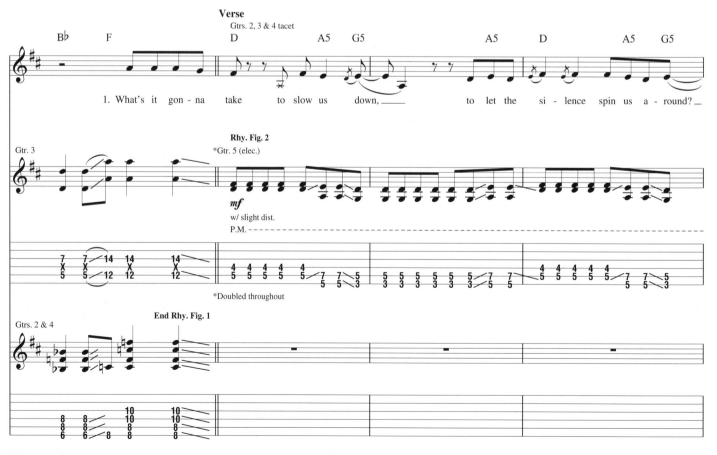

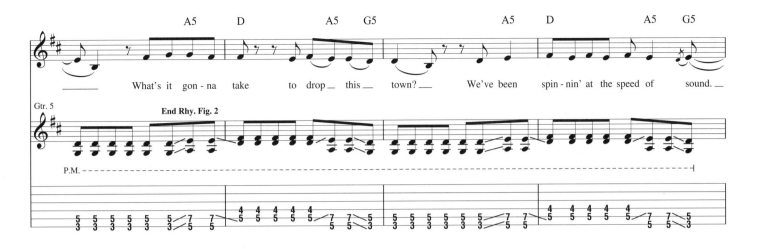

What's it gon-na take to drop_ this_ town?_ We've been spin-nin' at the speed of sound._

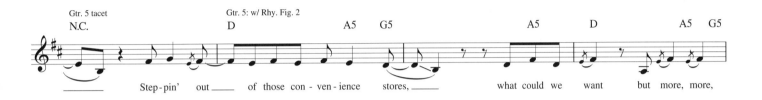

Step-pin' out ___ of those con-ven-ience stores, ___ what could we want but more, more,

more. _ From the third ___ world _ to the cor-p'rate core, _ we are the sym-pho-ny _

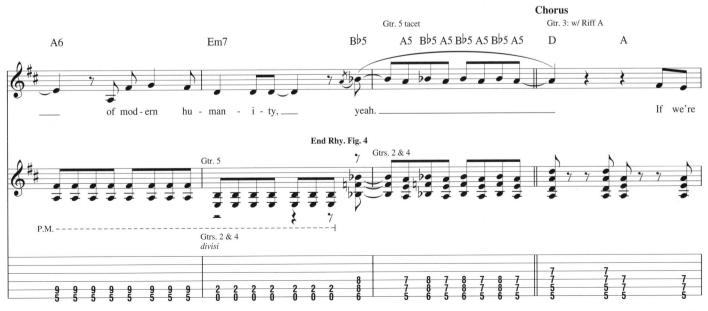

of mod-ern hu-man-i-ty, ___ yeah. ___ If we're

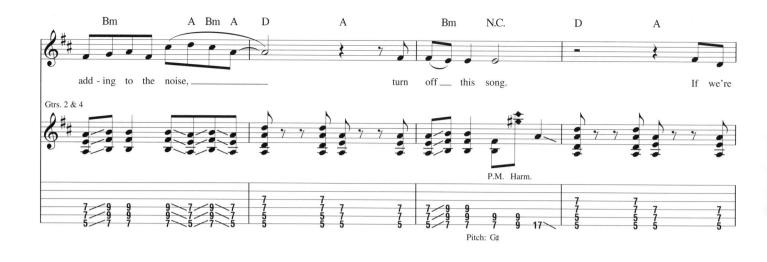

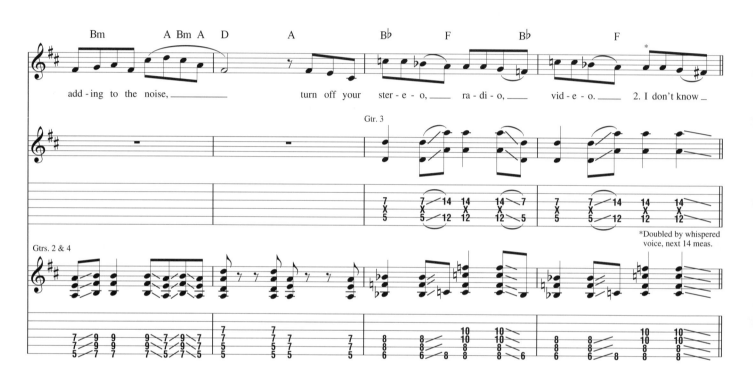

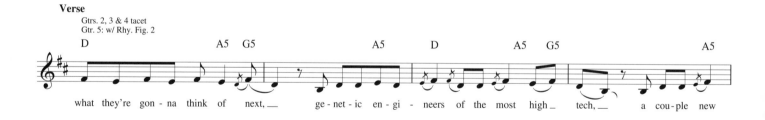

Verse

that TV___ set tells___ us what we want-ed to hear,___ but none of these

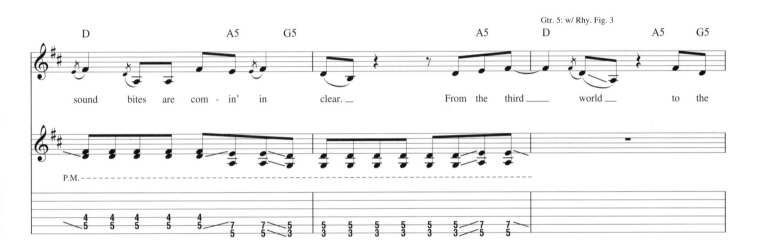

sound bites are com-in' in clear.___ From the third___ world___ to the

Pre-Chorus

cor - po - rate ear,___ we are the_____ sym - pho - ny___ of mod - ern hu -

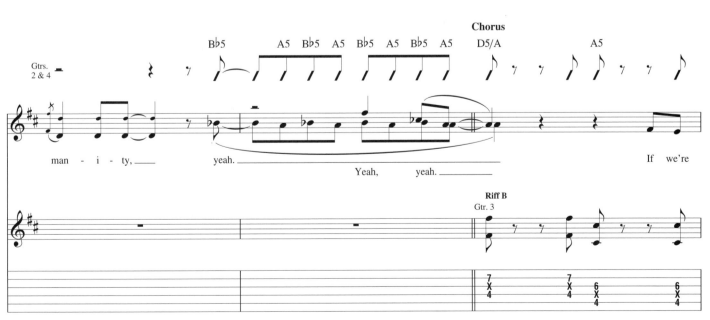

man - i - ty,___ yeah._____ If we're

Yeah, yeah.___

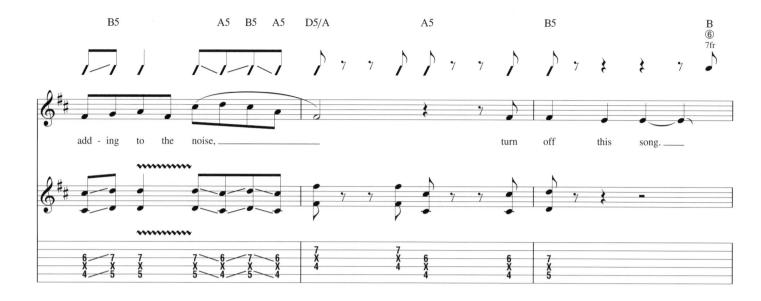

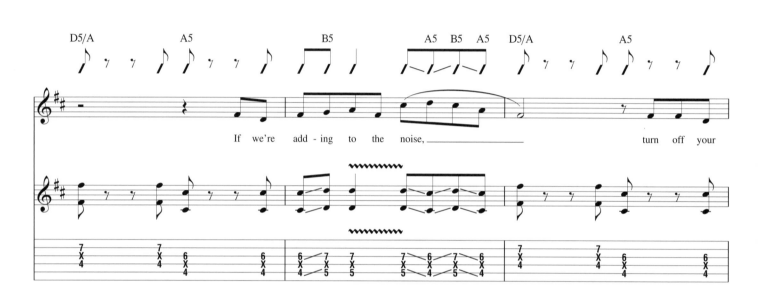

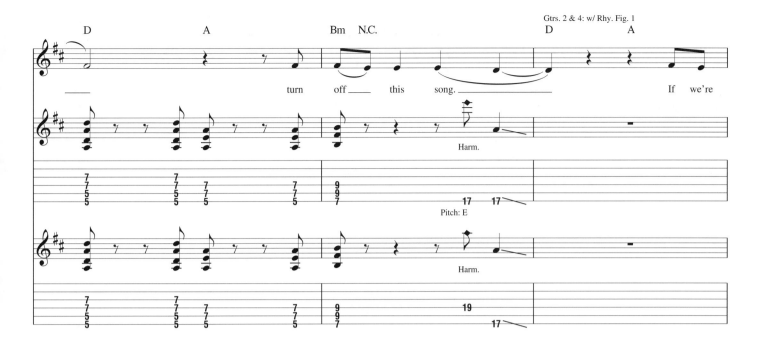

turn off ___ this song. ___ If we're

add - ing to the noise, ___ turn off your ster - e - o, ___ ra - di - o. ___

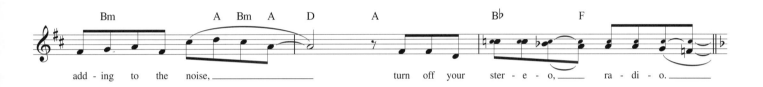

Bridge

*(Asus2) (Bsus4) (C#m7) (E)

Gtr. 6 (acous.)

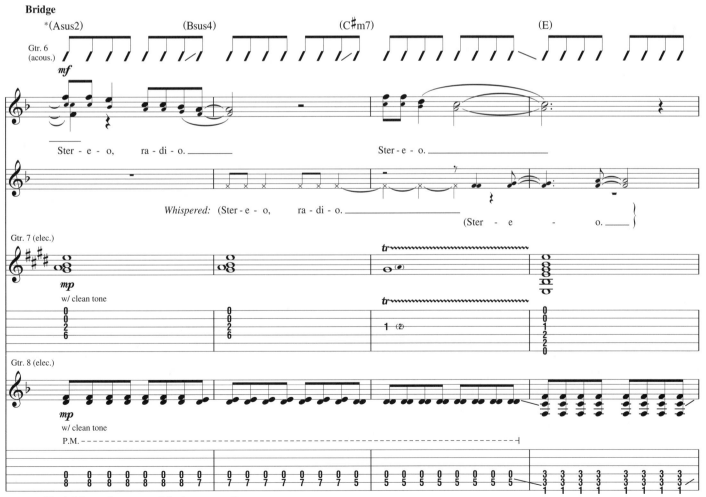

Ster - e - o, ra - di - o. ___ Ster - e - o. ___

Whispered: (Ster - e - o, ra - di - o. ___ (Ster - e - o. ___)

Gtr. 7 (elec.)

w/ clean tone

Gtr. 8 (elec.)

w/ clean tone

P.M. -

*Symbols in parentheses represent chord names respective
to capoed guitar and do not reflect actual pitch.

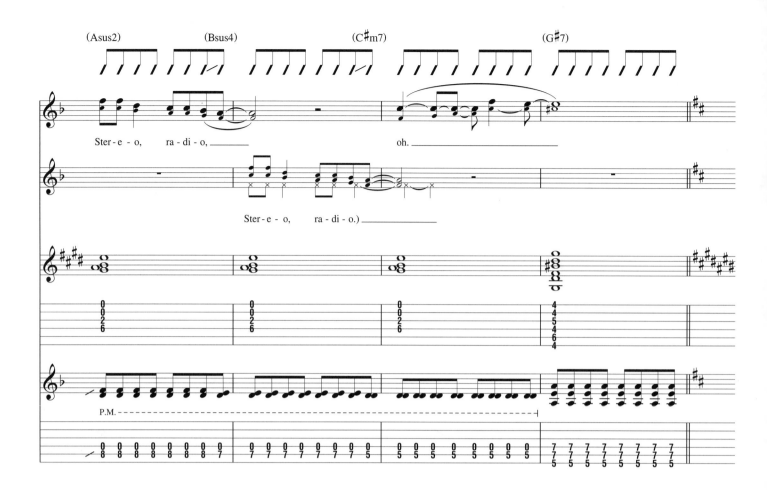

Ster - e - o, ra - di - o, _____ oh. _____

Ster - e - o, ra - di - o.) _____

P.M. ---

Chorus

Gtrs. 6, 7 & 8 tacet

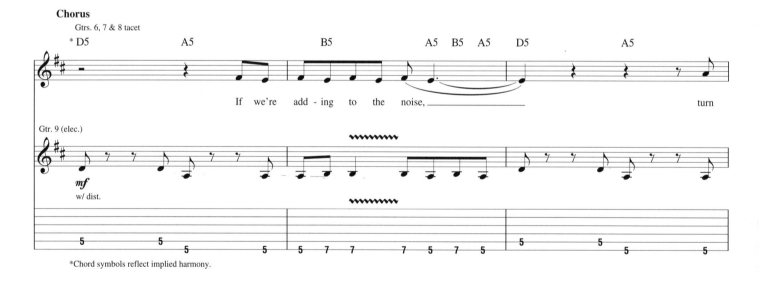

If we're add - ing to the noise, _____ turn

Gtr. 9 (elec.)

mf
w/ dist.

*Chord symbols reflect implied harmony.

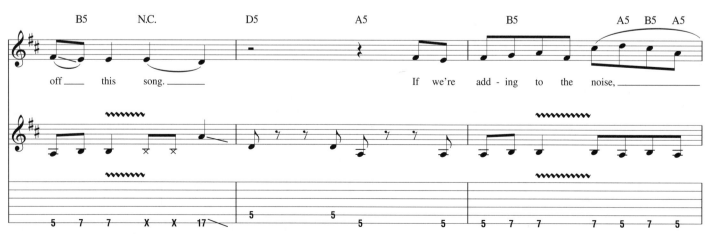

off _____ this song. _____ If we're add - ing to the noise, _____

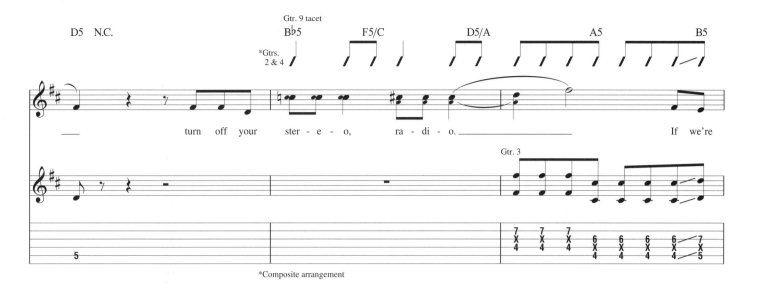

*Composite arrangement

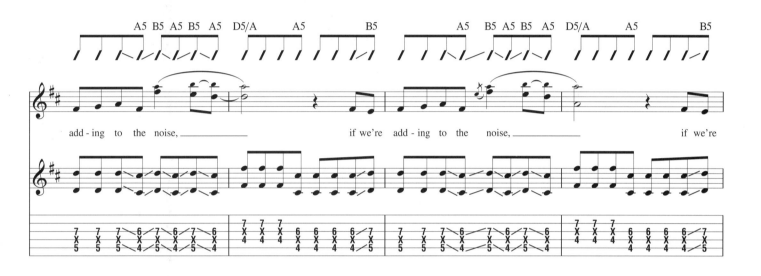

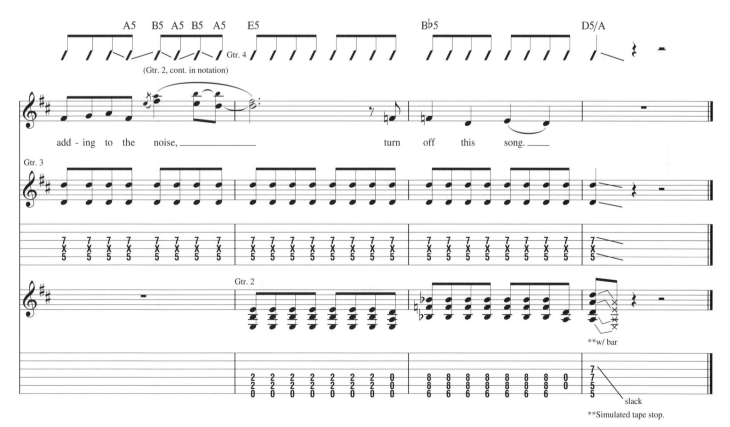

**w/ bar

slack

**Simulated tape stop.

Twenty-Four

Words and Music by Jonathan Foreman

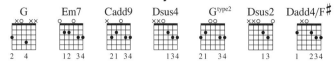

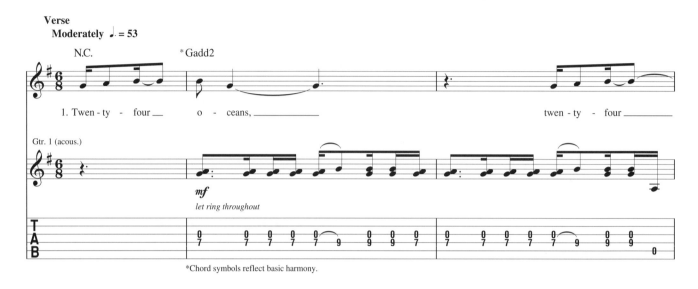

*Chord symbols reflect basic harmony.

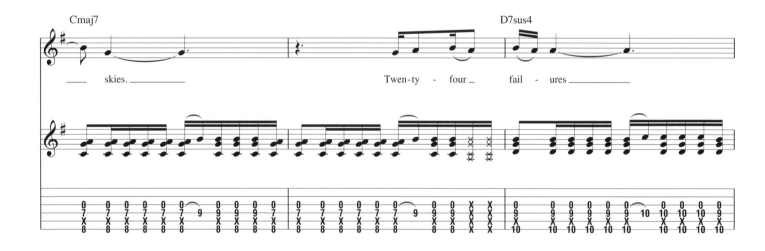

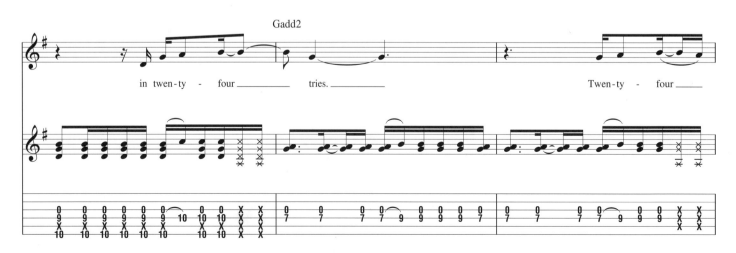

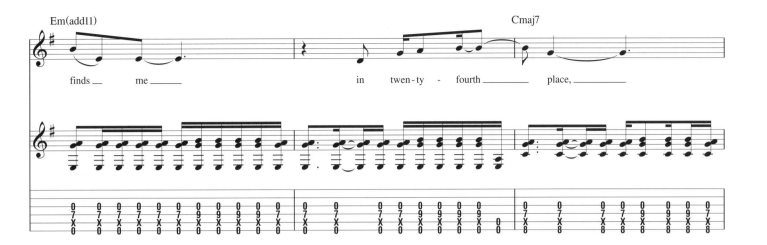

finds __ me _____ in twen-ty - fourth _____ place, _____

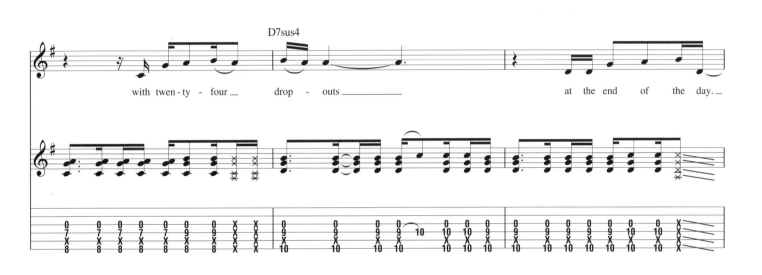

with twen-ty - four __ drop - outs _____ at the end of the day. __

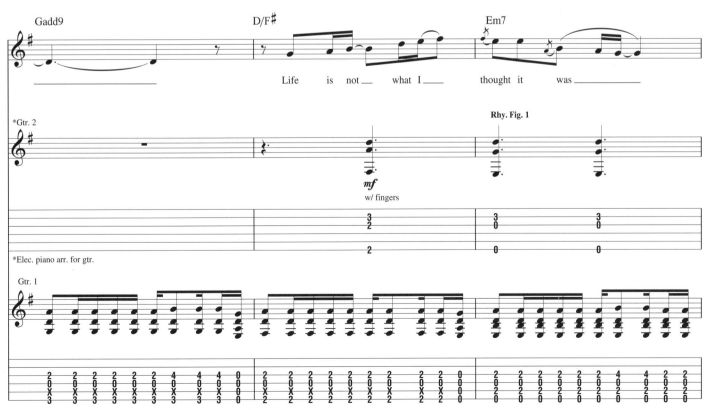

Life is not __ what I ____ thought it was _____

*Gtr. 2

Rhy. Fig. 1

mf
w/ fingers

*Elec. piano arr. for gtr.

Gtr. 1

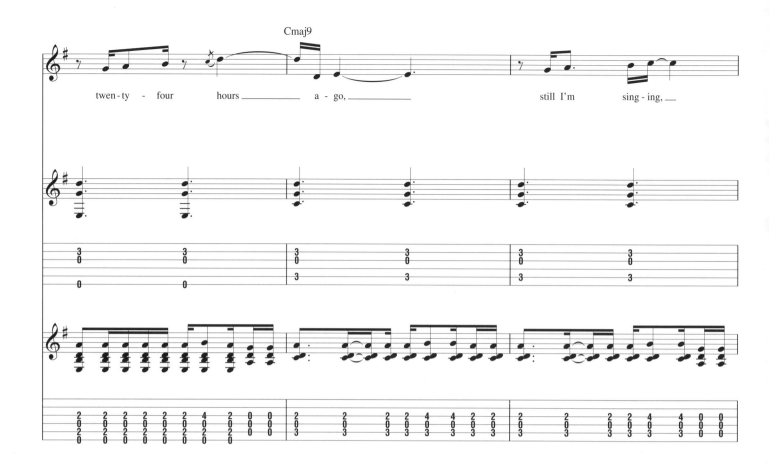

twen-ty - four   hours _____ a - go, _____   still I'm   sing - ing, __

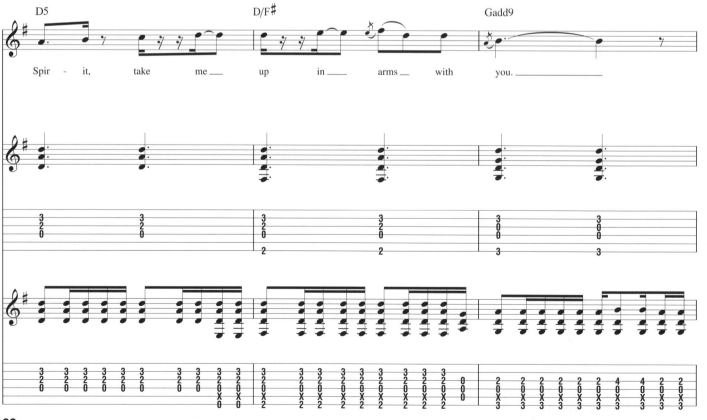

Spir - it,   take   me ___ up   in ___ arms ___ with   you. _____

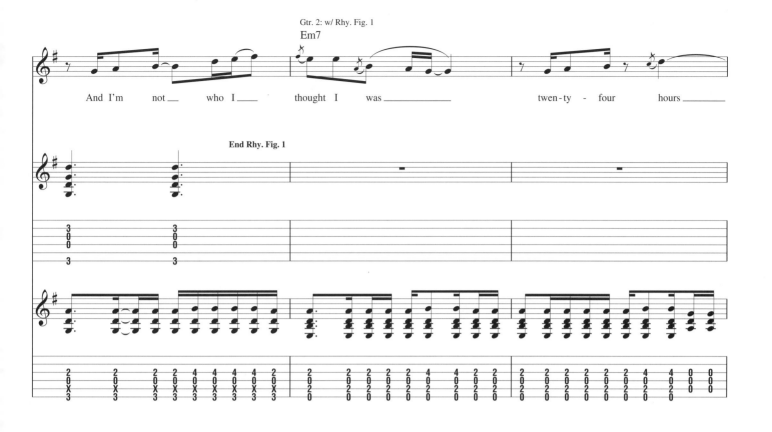

And I'm not__ who I__ thought I was _____ twen-ty - four hours _____

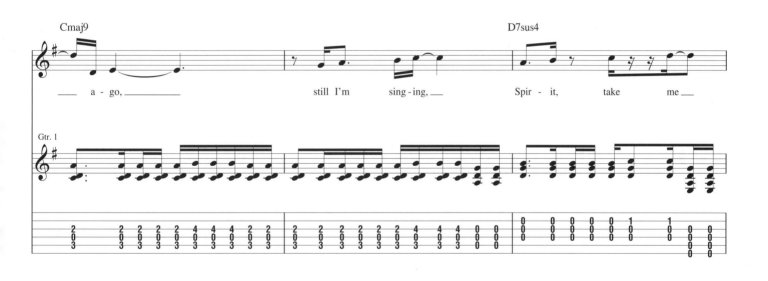

__ a - go, _____ still I'm sing-ing, __ Spir - it, take me __

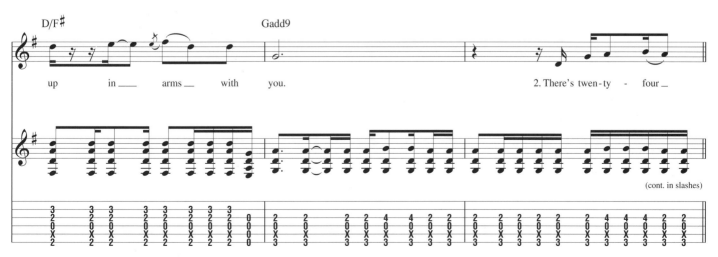

up in __ arms __ with you. 2. There's twen-ty - four __

(cont. in slashes)

Verse

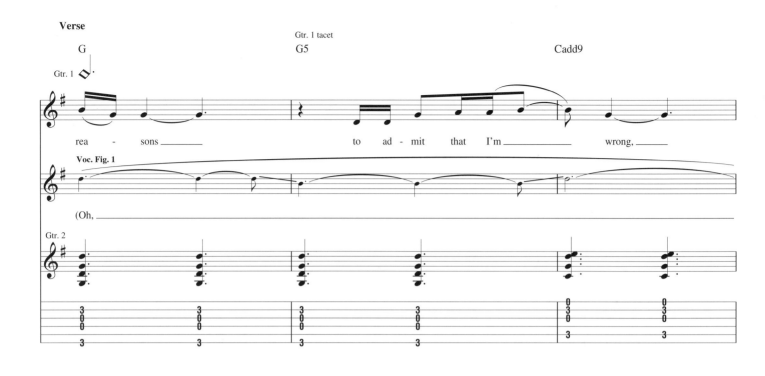

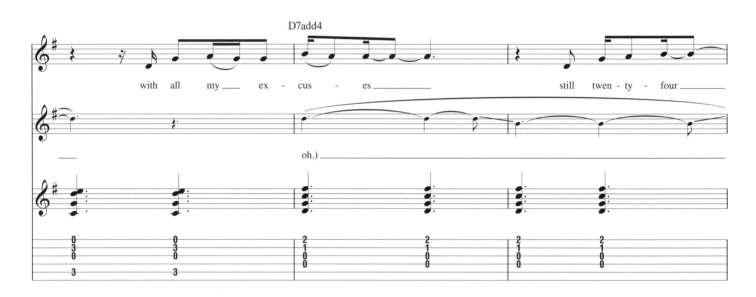

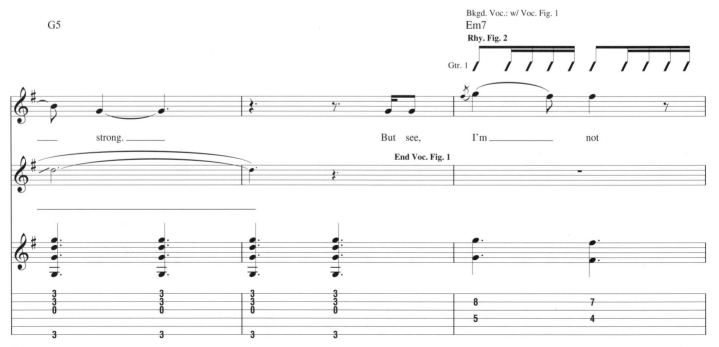

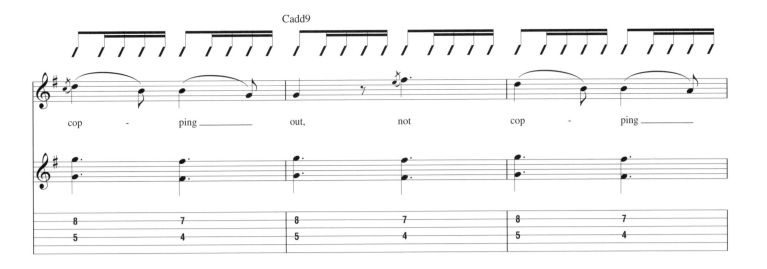

cop - ping ___ out, not cop - ping ___

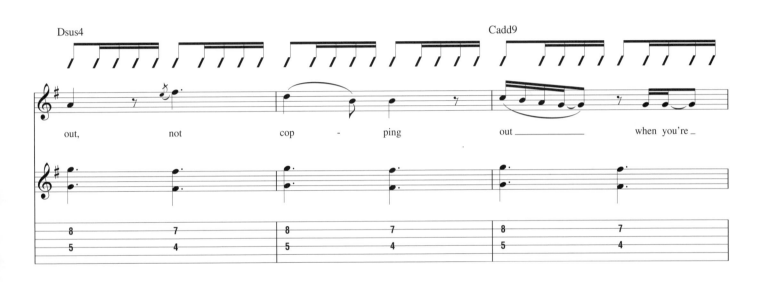

out, not cop - ping out ___ when you're ___

Chorus

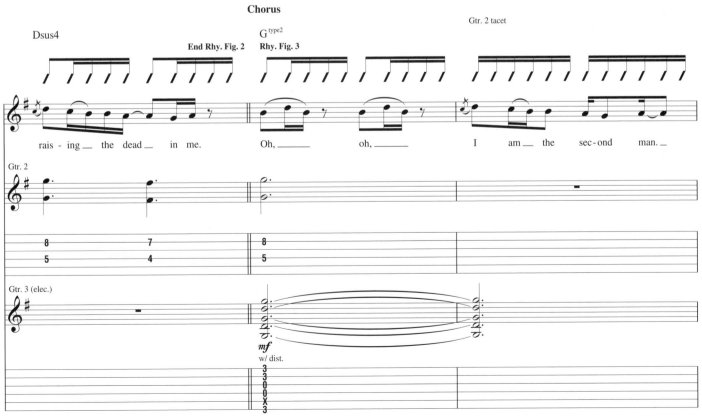

rais - ing ___ the dead ___ in me. Oh, ___ oh, ___ I am the sec - ond man.

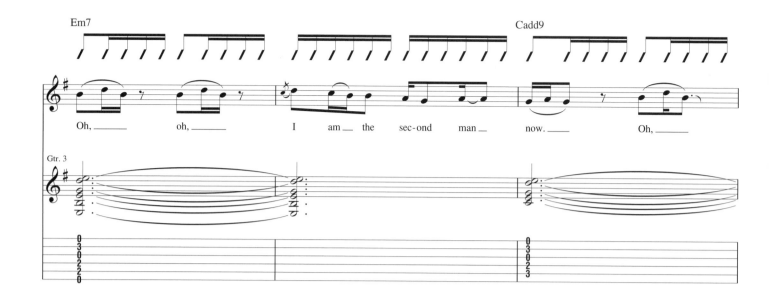

Oh, _____ oh, _____ I am _ the sec-ond man _ now. _____ Oh, _____

Gtr. 3

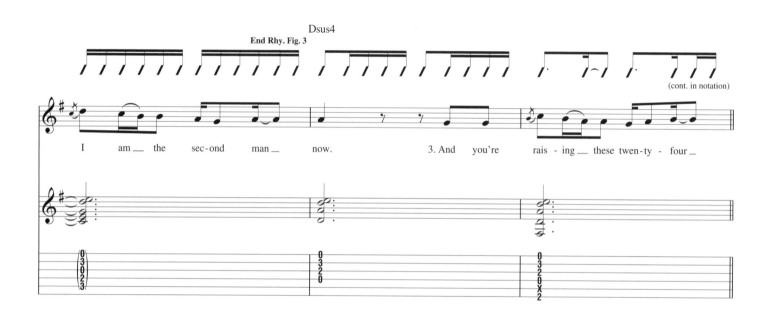

Dsus4

End Rhy. Fig. 3

(cont. in notation)

I am _ the sec-ond man _ now. 3. And you're rais-ing _ these twen-ty - four _

Verse

Gtr. 3 tacet

G

Em7

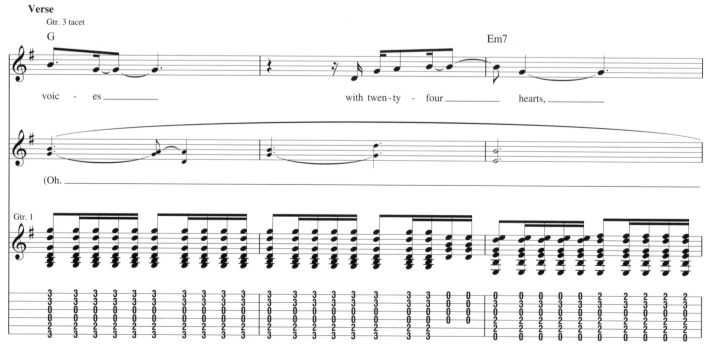

voic - es _____ with twen-ty - four _____ hearts, _____

(Oh. _____

Gtr. 1

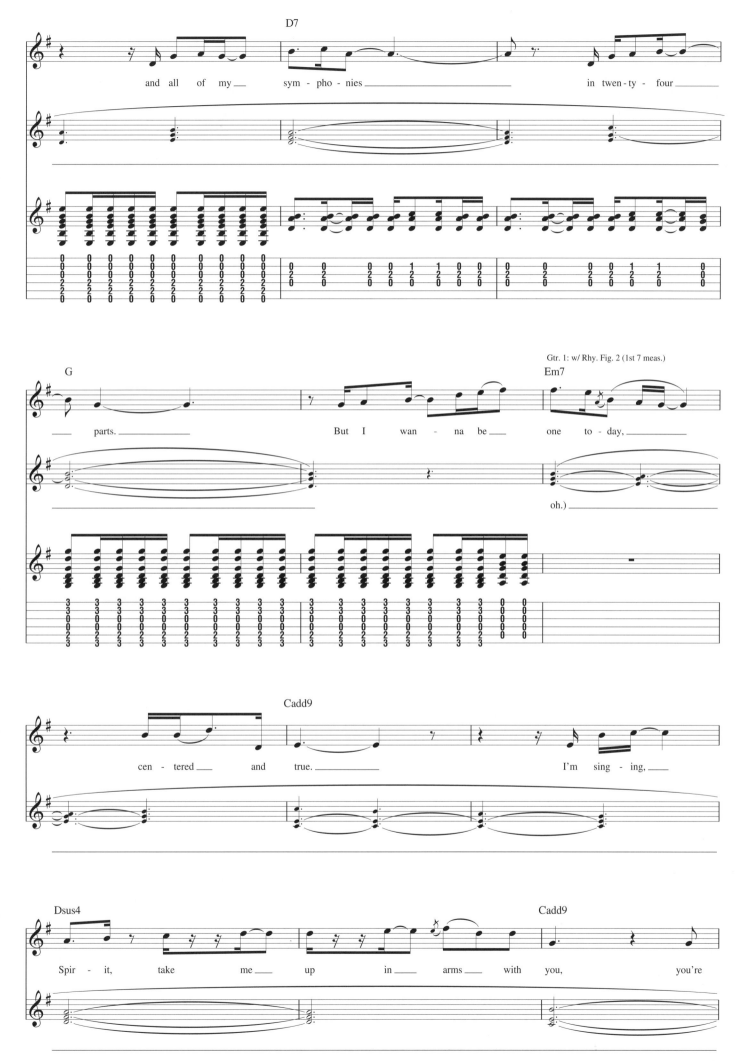

and all of my __ sym - pho - nies _____ in twen - ty - four __

__ parts. _____ But I wan - na be __ one to - day, _____

(oh.) _____

cen - tered __ and true. _____ I'm sing - ing, __

Spir - it, take me __ up in __ arms __ with you, you're

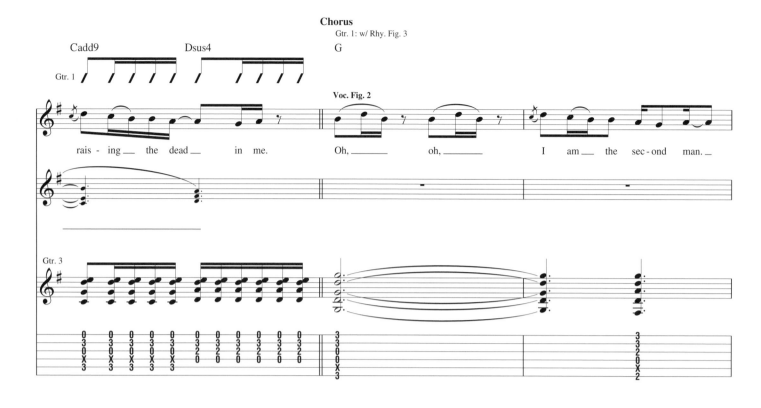

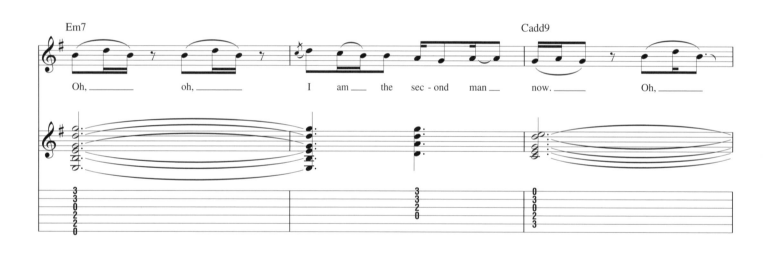

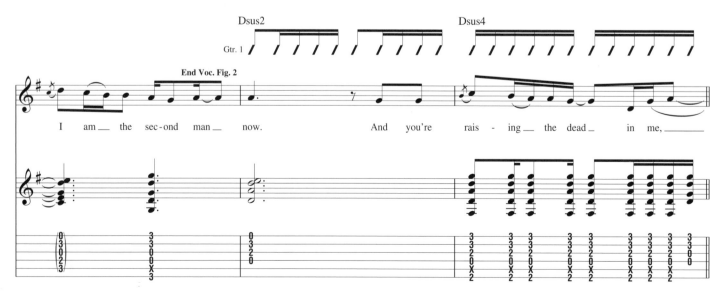

Interlude

Gtr. 1: w/ Rhy. Fig. 3

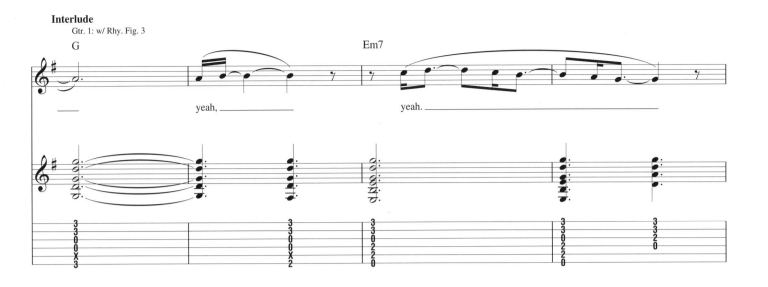

yeah, _____ yeah. _____

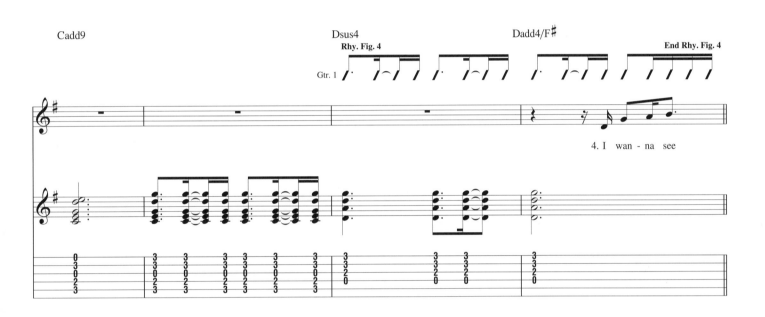

4. I wan - na see

Verse

Gtr. 3 tacet

Gtr. 1 tacet

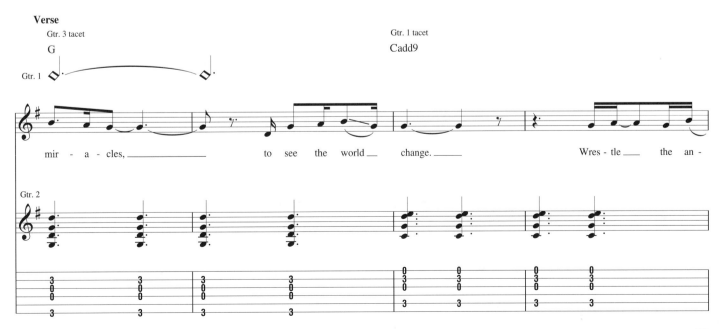

mir - a - cles, _____ to see the world ___ change. ___ Wres - tle ___ the an -

Outro-Chorus

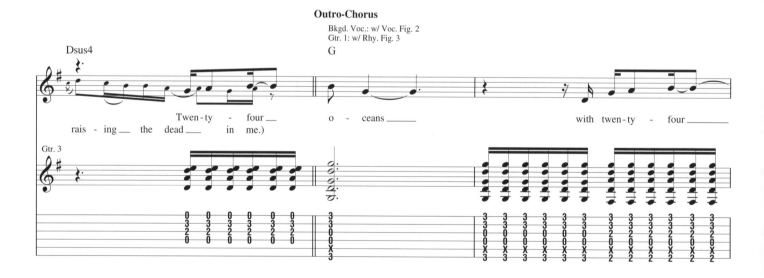

Gtr. 1: w/ Rhy. Fig. 4

Dsus4   Dadd4/F#

in twen-ty - four _____ parts. _____   Life is not _____ what I _____

Voc. Fig. 3   End Voc. Fig. 3

(...now. And you're rais - ing _____ the dead _____ in me.) _____

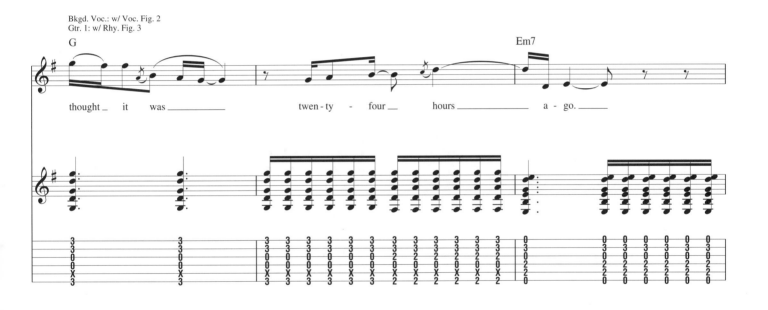

Bkgd. Voc.: w/ Voc. Fig. 2
Gtr. 1: w/ Rhy. Fig. 3

G   Em7

thought _____ it was _____ twen - ty - four _____ hours _____ a - go. _____

Cadd9

Still I'm sing - ing, _____   Spir - it, take _____ me _____ up in arms. _____

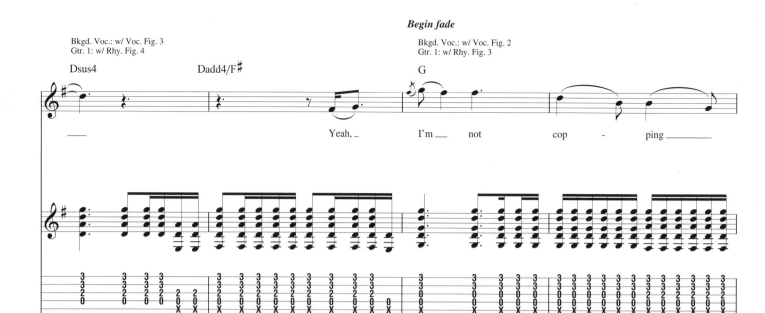

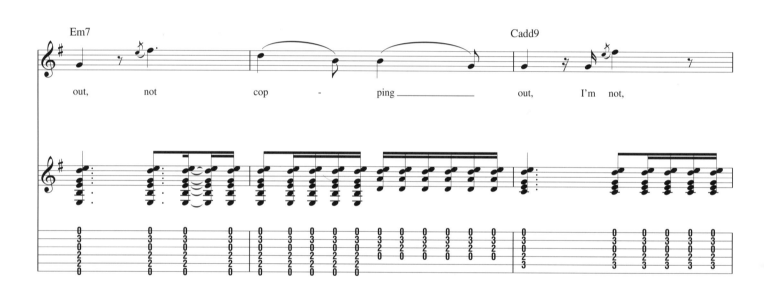

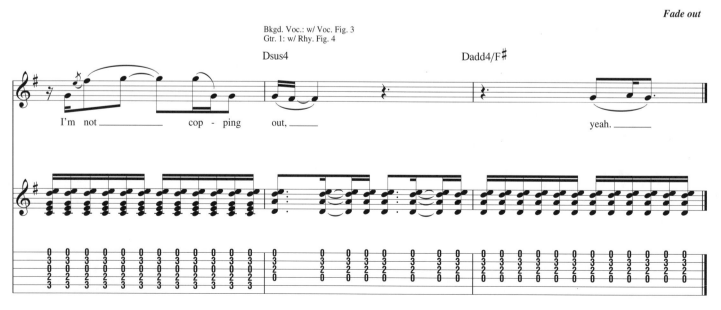